HEA

Higher Education Authority
An tÚdarás um Ard-Oideachas

THE PROGRAMME FOR RESEARCH IN THIRD LEVEL INSTITUTIONS [PRTLI] IMPACT ASSESSMENT - VOL I

REPORT BY THE INTERNATIONAL ASSESSMENT COMMITTEE

ISBN 0 - 904556 - 91 - 3

Dublin

Published by the Higher Education Authority

To be purchased from the
Government Publications Sales Office,
Molesworth Street, Dublin 2.

or through any Bookseller

Price €15
2004

STRUCTURE OF THE REPORT

This report is presented in two separate volumes:

- **VOLUME I** - The Main Report and Executive Summary

- **VOLUME II** - Supporting Documentation for the Committee prepared by independent consultants and the HEA.

TABLE OF CONTENTS

FOREWORD

The Higher Education Authority decided last July to establish an independent international Assessment Committee to conduct an independent impact assessment of the Programme for Research in Third Level Institutions (PRTLI). An in-depth and comprehensive review of the programme has now been completed by a distinguished international Assessment Committee. The first funding awards under PRTLI were made in 1999.

The review findings are set out in this report. The Assessment Committee considered progress by the PRTLI in meeting its objectives to the end of 2003. The review involved, over a period of 8 months, in the region of 100 international experts and peers, engaging with approximately 600 individuals in over 40 institutions and organisations. Site visits were held together with desk reviews, bibliometric analysis, data and information collation, interviews and meetings.

The HEA welcomes the fact that the Assessment Committee - **concluded** that the PRTLI is on its way to meeting all its objectives, **concluded** that the programme has had very positive impacts on institutional strategic planning, inter-institutional co-operation and on the quality of research being produced in Ireland, **endorses** the essential link between research and teaching and learning and **considers** the programme to be ambitious and farsighted.

The Government has set as a target that Ireland will be an innovation driven, knowledge economy. In that context, the acknowledgement in this Report that the programme has had a significant impact on the development of capabilities within the third level institutions is particularly important. The Report states '…we believe that PRTLI marks the beginning of a major and most beneficial transformation of the research landscape of Ireland that will help to install an innovation-driven economy'. The Report states that the Group are fully convinced about the merits and necessity of continued Government support for the programme.

There are also areas that the Group have highlighted that need further attention. In particular, at the institutional level, more effective sustainability planning by new PRTLI Centres and the need to embed a commercialisation ethos have been highlighted. There are recommendations for the Government, the HEA and the third level institutions, all of which need to be addressed to ensure continued progress and quality outcomes.

The HEA is most grateful to Prof. Enric Banda, currently director of the Catalan Research Foundation and former Secretary-General of the European Science Foundation (to end 2003), who chaired the Assessment Committee. We are also indebted to the other members of the group - Prof. Reijo Vihko (President of the Academy of Finland, to end March 2004), Prof. John Morrill (Professor of British and Irish History, Cambridge, UK and Acting Master of Selwyn College, Cambridge) and Prof. Lauren Resnick (Professor of Psychology and Director of the Institute for Learning, University of Pittsburgh, USA). The HEA appreciates the time and commitment the group gave to conducting this important review for Ireland.

The HEA also wishes to thank all of those who contributed as peer and expert reviewers to the programme and all of those individuals who met with the international committee, and those who contributed by making submissions to this process.

The Authority wishes to take this opportunity to express its gratitude to Atlantic Philanthropies for their generous support of this independent international assessment. The Authority also acknowledges that the financial support of Atlantic Philanthropies was of central importance in setting up PRTLI and the success of the programme. Their contribution is, in its generosity and foresight, without precedent in the Irish higher education sector.

The HEA looks forward to considering in detail the outcomes from this assessment and to working with the Minister for Education and Science, and with other Ministers and with their departments, to develop, the PRTLI so that it can best contribute to the further development of the Irish higher education and research system. The Authority also looks forward to working with the broad range of other stakeholders in the system, and to continuing the work of establishing Ireland as a recognised centre of excellence for education and research on the world stage.

DR DON THORNHILL
HEA CHAIRMAN
JUNE 2004

FUNDACIÓ
CATALANA
— PER A LA —
RECERCA

Director

Don Thornhill
Chairman
Higher Education Authority

Barcelona, 21st May 2004

Dear Chairman,   Dear Don

I am pleased to announce that the Steering Committee appointed to assess the results and performance of PRTLI has now finished its work. I am also glad to inform you that the Committee has been delighted with the help received from the HEA staff, the institutions and research staff, from the consultants and from the other people we have met. Of course, we are also happy with the necessary independence the Committee has had in carrying out its assessment.

From the outset, the Committee was attracted by the programme's unique characteristics, in particular, its strategic focus and the challenge to institutions to prioritise, its push for inter-institutional collaboration and its requirement for a stronger binding of research with the teaching and learning interface. This is an ambitious and farsighted design that we fully endorse.

The results to date, as outlined in our report, are persuasive. PRTLI is on its way to meeting all its objectives. In short, we believe that PRTLI marks the beginning of a major and most beneficial transformation of the research landscape of Ireland that will help to install an innovation-driven economy.

We are fully convinced about the merits of continued Government support for this unique initiative. We are strongly of the view that PRTLI is a good beginning, but only that. There is still much to do if Ireland is to close the gap with its more advanced European partners and contribute to the "Lisbon agenda".

Of course, we have found some aspects that need attention. In particular, the issues of intellectual property emerging from PRTLI and preparations for its commercialisation need to be addressed, as well as a more effective sustainability planning by the new PRTLI Centres. Finding non-bureaucratic structures that will improve the overall coherence of research funding at Government level, while retaining diversity, also stands out.

The Committee congratulates you and your Executive and the Authority on the impressive results that have been achieved so far. We wish you continued success in attracting the necessary public funding for the development of this unique and worthwhile programme.

With all best wishes,

Enric Banda
Chairman of the Assessment Committee

FUNDACIÓ CATALANA   Pg. Lluís Companys, 23   Telèfon 93 268 77 00   www.fcr.es
PER A LA RECERCA   08010 Barcelona   Telefax 93 315 01 40

PRTLI IMPACT
ASSESSMENT
COMMITTEE

From left – Professor Reijo Vihko, Professor Enric Banda, Professor Lauren B. Resnick and Professor John Morrill

Professor Enric Banda, Chairman. Director of the Catalan Research Foundation, Barcelona and member of the European Research Advisory Board. Formerly, Secretary General of the European Science Foundation, Research Professor of the Consejo Superior de Investigaciones Científicas (CSIC) and Director of its Earth Sciences Institute in Barcelona. Also acted as General Secretary of the Spanish National R+D Plan and Secretary of State for Universities and Research.

Professor Lauren B. Resnick, Professor of Psychology, University of Pittsburg and Director of the Learning Research and Development Center. Formerly member of the Commission on the Skills of the American Workforce and chair of the assessment committee of the SCANS Commission and of the Resource Group on Student Achievement of the National Education Goals Panel, member of the Commission on Behavioral and Social Sciences and Education and of the Mathematical Sciences Education Board at the National Research Council.

Professor John Morrill, Professor of British and Irish History, Cambridge University and Acting Master of Selwyn College, was Vice President of the British Academy (2000-2) and is currently a Member and Trustee of the UK Arts and Humanities Research Board and Chair of its Research Committee.

Professor Reijo Vihko, formerly President and Director General of the Academy of Finland, Professor of Chemical Pathology, member of the Finnish National Council for Science and Technology and of the Governing Council of the European Science Foundation, the World Health Organisation and currently chairman or member of the boards of a number of private companies in Finland.

EXECUTIVE SUMMARY

Introduction

We were delighted to accept the invitation by the Higher Education Authority to assess the impacts of this unique and farsighted initiative of the Irish Government.

In our experience, PRTLI is a remarkable endeavour. It breaks new ground in research funding schemes; especially in its focus on strengthening the linkages between teaching and research, its emphasis on institutional prioritisation of research investments and its support for institutions working together to create a more competitive critical mass of research effort. The integration of these features into a single funding scheme is what differentiates and gives a high profile to PRTLI and makes this initiative one of the most innovative that we have encountered.

Knowledge and intellectual capital will provide the foundations for the new innovation economy. This being so, Ireland must have both the ambition and the capacity to generate and to commercialise more of its own technology, domestically. A significant strengthening and development of advanced research and education capabilities will be central to the achievement of this important objective. In other words, Ireland must establish an internationally competitive '4th level' within its third level education system. PRTLI attempts to meet this objective. Following decades of relative impoverishment of the domestic research base, it represents a significant step forward in public research policy and in funding.

We perceive however that there is still much to be done to optimise the development of a knowledge-based Irish society. Notwithstanding the marked increases in research expenditures since the late 1990s – and particularly through PRTLI and SFI (Science Foundation Ireland) – expenditure on research in Ireland falls well short of international norms. Ireland is still playing 'catch-up', compared to other developed economies, especially in relation to the advanced sciences and technologies.

Our specific mandate was to assess whether the performance and results achieved to date are sufficient to show that the PRTLI initiative is on track and that it will satisfy its challenging objectives. We were greatly assisted in our task by excellent inputs from experienced international experts and consultants, by the beneficiary institutions, their staffs and students and by a wide range of other public and private stakeholders and interest groups, for which we express our deep appreciation.

For this interim assessment, we thoroughly examined the quality of the research supported by PRTLI. We have also examined the response of the institutions to PRTLI's strategic and management requirements and the effectiveness of the linkages between PRTLI funded research and the teaching and learning environments for third level students, undergraduate and postgraduate. We have reviewed where PRTLI fits into the overall funding regime for research in Ireland and related research funding bodies, as well as the continuing relevance of its underlying aims and objectives.

Achievements and Impacts to Date

Based on the extensive evidence that has been supplied to us by independent consultants and on our own investigations and site visits, it is our view and the overwhelming view of all visiting experts from outside Ireland, that the investment in PRTLI is fully justified and should be continued.

Very significant levels of PRTLI research funding are now being strategically and effectively deployed on a priority basis by institutions that are beginning to adopt a more professional approach to research organisation, planning and management. Research quality, scale of operations, and critical mass are being achieved. Remarkable advances are being made in getting institutions to work together, including the institutes of technology. We have seen strong evidence of an emerging collaborative culture between all these institutions, most of which have hitherto worked in isolation. The diversity of scientific disciplines, across all institutions that are being focused on common goals, is impressive. The unique PRTLI model seems destined to produce very highly skilled personnel for the national economy, as well as radically new scientific insights, if this level of interdisciplinarity is maintained. Teaching and learning environments for third level students are being enhanced with a significantly closer binding at the interface between research and teaching.

The external experts, all from outside Ireland, were impressed with the general trends in PRTLI publications output and impact, and we share this view. Designed to promote world-class research across all disciplines, there is evidence that PRTLI is succeeding in this in the Humanities and Social Sciences, as well as in the Sciences and Engineering. Although Irish publication output is still low in comparison with other comparable EU countries, it is increasing steadily. It is too early to assess the full impacts of PRTLI funding in terms of research outputs, but impacts thus far in all fields are in the category of 'high to very high', and the bibliometric assessment shows that the impact of papers by PRTLI researchers is higher than the national average.

If the programme continues to deliver this performance, and provided the level of investment is sustained, we are satisfied that Ireland will be well on the way to creating a very strong and internationally competitive '4th level' education and research sector that will drive its ambitions for achieving a knowledge and innovation intensive economy. We reckon that the results achieved to date are all the more remarkable, considering that PRTLI is still at a relatively early stage of development, with a drawdown to date of only 37% of the funds approved.

The PRTLI process itself is generally perceived as satisfactory – "unusual by international standards, but a very fair process". Its integrity is widely respected by the institutions and the independence of the international assessment panel in project selection is, in our view, one of its outstanding strengths. We commend the Authority and its executive for their non-interventionist approach and for the establishment of a truly competitive process committed to supporting excellent research.

However, all examiners and reviewers have expressed the view, which we endorse, that the important goals of PRTLI will be achieved only if funding on a significant scale is sustained over an extended period – in our view, for at least another ten years.

Areas for Improvement

The positive nature of our general conclusions about PRTLI is not without some concerns, however.

Our major concern at this juncture is about the sustainability of PRTLI funded centres and the inadequate attention that generally is given to sustainability planning by most of the new centres. There is virtually no business planning in these and overhead provision, currently at 15%, is wholly inadequate. In our view, this ought to be about 45%. We understand from discussions with the institutions that some cross subsidisation may be required to enable continuation of ongoing levels of activity, but we would be concerned that this may hurt the teaching domain and other non-PRTLI areas of institutional responsibility.

We are also aware that uncertainties about the stability of future funding have damaged confidence in the Government's commitment to staying the course. The testimony of stakeholders and industry representatives on this point was consistently strong and insistent. In our experience, continuity and consistency in core public funding will be essential to sustain these new PRTLI centres and to regain international confidence that was lost as a consequence of the year long 'pause' in 2003, now happily resolved.

In our discussions we noted concerns about the extent to which PRTLI addressed issues related to enterprise and industrial policy and regarding its exact positioning within the national system of innovation. We also noted inadequate resourcing by the institutions themselves of arrangements for intellectual property rights (IPR) and commercialisation. Though matters are improving, our visiting experts expressed concerns at the adequacy of training in IPR and in IPR protection and management.

Notwithstanding PRTLI's explicit avoidance of commercial and near to market research, which we support, we feel that it is necessary to more clearly define its position and role within the national innovation system in Ireland. If this were done, it would enable the more effective engagement of PRTLI with research funding programmes outside the education sector, and if achieved, would help to bring about a greater national coherence in research funding policies and programmes, generally. We have a serious concern about this lack of coherence in research funding arrangements, because it threatens not only PRTLI, but also the whole research edifice, if it is not attended to.

We believe also, that the strategic dimension of PRTLI continues to be very important, because it demands a careful assessment by the institutions themselves of the external environment in which they operate, including consideration of the business and enterprise policy agenda and its needs. We would like to see a stronger consideration by the institutions of this particular element of strategic planning in future and believe that it will help to more securely position PRLTI and its contribution within the national innovation system. We feel also, that private sector 'pull' can be expected when the true potential of the capabilities being established in third level institutions is fully appreciated and we had some evidence from our interviews with industrial representatives that interest is already beginning to show in the advanced technology sectors.

Our concern about coherence in research funding extends especially to the relationship between PRTLI and SFI. In our view, and from the evidence of our investigations, there is a mutual synergy between the two, which needs to be better managed. We are strongly of the view that PRTLI provides the backbone on which specific initiatives like SFI and others depend and can be made effective and we have noted a significant and welcome synergy between recent SFI investments and earlier allocations under PRTLI. But we are not convinced from what we have seen and heard that this relationship is managed in the most effective way within the existing government structures.

We feel that more can be achieved on the teaching and learning connection. The initial gains which have been substantial have been in more and better education offerings, stronger engagement of postgraduates in research and wider exposure of students to the research environment. The next must come from new and innovative teaching methods, improved instruction tools and new learning environments and, more generally, through quality improvements in the teaching and learning process itself, as much as in volume of new programme offerings. PRTLI now needs to address the development of more innovative linkages and new binding mechanisms at the research and teaching interface.

Finally, at the level of the institutions, there is a key challenge to resolve the relationship between the new PRTLI centres and the traditional departmental structure of the institutions. Some very major centres reported to us difficulties in overcoming departmental resistance in top-level recruitment, for example. We are aware that this is not a settled relationship and we fear that the issue is not receiving the urgent consideration that it needs in most institutions. Clearly, this issue needs to be addressed as a matter of urgency.

Recommendations

Our detailed recommendations are outlined in Chapter 6. These are aimed at Government, the institutions and the HEA. In summary terms, these are:

For Government

- We strongly recommend consistent and sustained investment in this Programme by the Irish Government over the period of the current National Plan and its continuation for at least a further 10-year planning period.

- We recommend that the Government continue to support a flexible and diverse funding system for third level institutions in Ireland; a system that underpins the highest quality teaching and learning in the institutions and that motivates and enables multiple research opportunities and potentials.

- We recommend the establishment of the necessary arrangements to bring about improved coherence in research funding. We favour the establishment of a supervisory body at the highest level (Taoiseach's Department) with participation of the major funding agencies, with the aims of ensuring coherence and retaining diversity in funding policies and programmes. It should be independently chaired, ideally by the Taoiseach, and not by a sectoral minister. A transversal committee, chaired at the highest level, will help to produce the necessary coherence in funding, as good practice in other countries demonstrates. However, these arrangements should be administratively thin and flexible and avoid any new and heavy bureaucracy.

For the Institutions

- We recommend the introduction of business planning for all newly established PRTLI centres and its requirement for all future funding applications under PRTLI.

- In general, the institutions must pay greater attention to the commercial and business potential of investments made under the PRTLI. We recommend that the IPR arrangements in all institutions be strengthened and better resourced by the colleges.

- We recommend that all institutions in receipt of PRTLI funding for new centres should now specifically define the responsibility, authority and accountability parameters that will determine the desired relationship between these new centres and the traditional structures of the institutions. This issue will not resolve itself and will create tensions if allowed to drift. It merits the urgent attention of senior management in the institutions.

- Also, in relation to management, we recommend more management training for centre managers and opportunities for managers at different institutions to exchange information about effective management practices.

- We also recommend regular review of strategic planning at the institutions in order to assist the further focusing of activities in areas of strength and /or important emergent fields of research.

- We strongly encourage the institutes of technology to continue their participation in PRTLI, but we are against a two-tier PRTLI and therefore, we recommend against any relaxation of institutional competition or any ringfencing arrangements that would preferentially favour institute of technology participation.

For the HEA

- We recommend a greater focus on people and equipment in the next round of PRTLI funding and rather less than heretofore on buildings – though some institutions still struggle with large infrastructural deficits, which should be corrected.

- We recommend that institutions in receipt of earlier PRTLI funding must meet, *inter alia*, demanding performance criteria, to be specified and monitored by the HEA, in order to be eligible for further PRTLI support.

- We recommend continuation of the institutional and strategic focus of PRTLI, together with a more explicit consideration of the industrial policy agenda and priorities in the formulation of institutional strategies for research.

- We recommend that HEA undertakes a specific study of the innovation system, from the perspective of research and education, to determine how best to improve the connections between PRTLI and the economic and industrial policy agendas of the relevant Government Departments and agencies.

- In regard to the PRTLI process, we recommend that the HEA

- improves the feedback process and the content of information provided to applicant institutions,

- considers the introduction of *vivas* or other face-to-face opportunities for applicants to present proposals to assessors,

- establishes a consistent set of indicators that will be used for programme monitoring. The indicators developed for this study may provide a basis for this.

- We recommend that HEA undertakes a study of the opportunities for inter-institutional education programmes.

- We recommend that the public relations side of the Programme be considerably strengthened. Possibly also, HEA ought to consider a change of name for the Programme. PRTLI is not well known or appreciated outside the education sector and ways of strengthening its 'corporate image' need to be addressed.

- In recognition of the interim nature of this report, we recommend that HEA undertake a further assessment of PRTLI in 3 to 5 years time, including bibliometric assessments and building on the data assembled for this study.

1 | BACKGROUND TO THE ASSESSMENT COMMITTEE'S CONSIDERATION OF PRTLI

1.1 Introduction

Every country has its own unique capabilities and potentials, as well as its policies for developing them. Yet, one thing is clear. As economies become more knowledge intensive, the nations that prosper are those that pay special attention to their resources of knowledge capital, as developed by and through research, technology, education and especially by advanced human capital. These have become the drivers of national innovation systems and the determinants of competitive advantage in international trade.

The implications are obvious. Without sustained accumulation and deployment of indigenous knowledge capital, the growth of small and very open trading nations, like Ireland, will be held back.

Higher education institutions, with their capacity for research and their commitment to the enhancement of human capital, have become the central players in most European countries in the drive to accumulate and exploit knowledge capital. In this regard, recent Irish policy to support this sector strongly is entirely consistent with the needs of Irish society and with current European ambitions and plans.

1.2 The Programme for Research in Third Level Institutions (PRTLI)

The Committee understands that the Programme for Research in Third Level Institutions (PRTLI) now occupies a central position in Government strategy for development of "world class research environment in our higher education institutions...."[1]. Established as a public/private partnership with the generous support of Atlantic Philanthropies, an international philanthropic organisation with a base in Ireland, the fundamental purpose of this unique and farsighted initiative is to build internationally competitive and collaborative research centres in a number of third level institutions and to network them globally, thereby enhancing the quality and availability of human capital for the Irish economy.

Some €698 million is earmarked in the National Development Plan for the period 2000 to 2006 to support research and technology across a wide spectrum in the education sector. We appreciate that the scale of this commitment marks a watershed in public policy towards research in third level institutions in Ireland.

1.3 Developing Knowledge Capital

Realisation that the Irish economy would greatly benefit from a shift from its traditional dependence on foreign investment and imported technology to generating more of its own technology domestically - from being an investment driven to becoming an innovation driven economy – appears now to be well established. One of the first results from investment in domestic knowledge production would be an increase in the capacity of knowledge absorption by society at large.

---

1. National Development Plan 2000-2006.

The resulting development of indigenous research capabilities, especially in third level institutions, will drive the transition to a knowledge based and innovation driven economy.

We understand that the remarkable growth of the Irish economy during the 1990s has helped to provide the resources for this. However, the return to more conventional growth rates in recent years brings a new challenge to sustain the investments already made under PRTLI and to maintain the momentum of the past five years. Any uncertainty in this regard would jeopardise the substantial investments and major progress that have already been made under PRTLI, as well as under other related initiatives supporting research and education.

There is still much to be done therefore, to optimise the development of a knowledge-based Irish society. Notwithstanding the marked increases in research expenditures since the late 1990s – and particularly through PRTLI and SFI (Science Foundation Ireland) – expenditure on research in Ireland still falls well short, compared to most EU-15 countries. Ireland is still playing 'catch-up', compared to other developed economies, especially in relation to the advanced sciences and technologies[2]. The GERD/GDP targets set in Barcelona in 2002 (3%) demonstrate the magnitude of the challenge facing the Irish Government (Ireland is now at 1.17% of GDP)[3]. PRTLI marks the start of Government efforts to address this challenge.

Against this background the Committee has set about its task of determining whether the interim performance and results of the PRTLI initiative provides enough evidence that the Programme is on track and that it will satisfy the demanding objectives set for it.

2. The indicator data in Volume 2 shows the magnitude of the challenge facing the Irish universities. The research income of the University of Edinburgh in 2002 was four times bigger than University College Cork. The University of Uppsala had a research income in 2003 six times the size of Trinity College Dublin. University College London has a research income eight times bigger than University College Dublin. Compared to two mainstream Dutch universities, in 2003, University College Dublin's per capita research income was one third of the University of Leiden and one quarter that of the University of Utrecht.
3. The latest available data is for 2001. Research and Development in Ireland 2001. Forfas, Dublin 2003.

2 | AIMS AND OBJECTIVES OF PRTLI

2.1 Origins and Scope

The Programme for Research in Third Level Institutions (PRTLI) is a government initiative to support high quality basic research in third level institutions in Ireland.

The Programme has been in operation since 1998 and is currently funded under the National Development Plan 2000-2006, with assistance from the European Regional Development Fund and with private funding through a public/private financial framework.

Funding is available to support all sectors and disciplines, at the discretion of applicant institutions.

Funding is allocated to eligible institutions on a competitive basis. Applicant institutions must satisfy demanding criteria as regards contributing to realising the goals and objectives of their strategic policy and plans for research, thereby enhancing their long-term research capacity and developing critical mass in priority sectors and disciplines.

To date, a total of €605 million has been approved, for both capital and current funding, to 23 out of a total of 35 eligible institutions – 15 receive funds as lead institutions and 8 as partner institutions. €186 million came from private sources[4]. A total of 62 research programmes, covering science and engineering, social sciences, humanities and library services have been supported. Three universities have secured more than €100 million each – University College Cork €123 million, University College Dublin €111 million and Trinity College Dublin €109 million.

The administration of the Programme and the allocation of funds are co-ordinated by the Higher Education Authority (HEA) on behalf of the Department of Education and Science.

Details of PRTLI funding allocations are provided in Volume II, Supporting Documentation.

2.2 Aims and Objectives

PRTLI is concerned with building a sustainable, long-term and broadly-based research capability in third level institutions through the establishment of internationally competitive research centres. Its intention is to accelerate the development of critical mass in existing strengths and to develop new areas consistent with their institutional strategies and plans for research. Uniquely, it also seeks a close linkage between research and the quality of teaching and learning at all levels in the institution.

In pursuit of its mission within the education sector, it seeks primarily to develop an advanced level of human capital through world-class research.

Philanthropies.

Specifically, the objectives of PRTLI are:

- To enable a strategic and planned approach by third level institutions to the long-term development of their research capabilities, consistent with their research missions and with their existing and developing research strengths and capabilities.

- To promote the development of high quality research capabilities in third-level institutions, so as to enhance the quality and relevance of graduate and postgraduate output and skill at all levels.

- Within the framework of these objectives, to provide support for outstandingly talented individual researchers and teams within institutions and the encouragement of co-operation between researchers both within the institutions and between institutions – having regard to the desirability of encouraging inter-institutional co-operation within and between the two parts of the binary system and within Ireland, the EU and internationally.

PRTLI's origins derive from the HEA's and the Department of Education and Science's perception of the need to:

- Strengthen institutional capacity for advanced research and assist institutions to establish selected world class centres of research excellence, consistent with their institutional strengths and capabilities.

- Strengthen the synergies between research and education in the formation of human capital and in the development of a world class '4th level' in Ireland through a closer binding of advanced research and the research mindset with teaching, learning and education.

- Promote and embed inter-institutional collaboration between third level institutions in order to counterbalance the comparative limitations of scale in the Irish higher education research system.

- Encourage the development of a more strategic approach by the institutions by providing support for the implementation and achievement of institutional strategies for research, as well as assisting those institutions willing to establish efficient and effective research management arrangements.

In our experience, these central features of PRTLI set it apart from other research funding schemes nationally. Even internationally, there is little to compare with it. The difference lies in its effort to bind the research and teaching linkage more effectively, its emphasis on institutional strategies and prioritisation and its focus on inter-institutional collaboration within the third level sector. Fundamentally, it focuses on the formation and development of human capabilities and the growth of a strong '4th level' capability in Irish third level education. The resulting policies and structures form a firm basis for global interaction and networking

3 | TERMS OF REFERENCE AND PROCEDURES OF THE ASSESSMENT

3.1 Terms of Reference

This is an interim assessment of the progress and performance of PRTLI since its inception in 1998[5]. Our basic aim was to establish what progress PRTLI is making towards the establishment of an internationally competitive research capacity in the eligible institutions, if it is performing according to plan and if its operation is consistent with its stated objectives. We also sought to identify any interim adjustments that might be necessary to improve its efficiency and effectiveness.

Capability building programmes like this that are targeted at basic research take time to mature and especially if, like PRLTI, they involve significant new building investments. It will be some years therefore, before the full and hopefully, ever increasing impacts of PRTLI can be estimated. Nonetheless, after not more than five years of operation, the evidence of the performance of the Programme is emerging and it is possible to discern the signals that indicate what final results are likely to be achieved.

For this interim assessment, we thoroughly examined the quality of the research supported by PRTLI, using a variety of techniques. We have also examined the response of the institutions to PRTLI's strategic and management requirements and the effectiveness of the linkages between PRTLI funded research and the teaching and learning environments for third level students, undergraduate and postgraduate. We have also examined where PRTLI fits into the overall funding regime for research in Ireland and related research funding bodies, as well as the continuing relevance of its underlying aims and objectives.

The full terms of reference for the work of the Committee are provided in Appendix B.

3.2 Procedures

Our findings are based on our extensive consultations with stakeholders and participants, government and industry representatives, beneficiary institutions and their top management and with the principal investigators and researchers undertaking the programme. We visited extensively the participating institutions and were assisted in our investigations by a range of inputs from independent consultants, international experts and peers.

We:

- Conducted our own analysis and visited all the major PRTLI funded institutions, inspected research facilities and interviewed the heads and senior management of these institutions.

- Met with a cross section of unsuccessful PRLTI applicants.

- Interviewed a wide range of other stakeholder interests, including representatives of all the relevant government departments and agencies, research funding bodies, business and industry representatives and the private donor.

---

3. The programme is still in its early stages - of the €605 million approved only €223 million (37%) has so far been drawn down by the institutions.

- Reviewed and were guided by the results of specially commissioned consultancy reports on research quality. These were based on the findings of experts from outside Ireland who visited and inspected selected research sites and programmes, a specially commissioned peer assessment of the international quality of a sample of PRTLI publications and a bibliometrics analysis carried out by specialists in this field[6].

- Reviewed and were guided by the results of specially commissioned consultancy reports on institutional strategy and management, policy and collaboration impacts of PRTLI[7].

- Reviewed a range of performance indicators developed jointly by the consultants, with assistance from the HEA.

- Held two briefings for members of the Higher Education Authority, including one by video link and briefed senior political interests on the preliminary findings.

The Committee met three times, including a week-long meeting and site visits during February 2004 and held sessions in private, as needed. It was fully facilitated in carrying out its remit in an independent and objective manner.

Details of the visiting experts and peer reviewers are provided in Appendix C and a full listing of all interviewees is provided in Appendix D.

---

6. Provided by The CIRCA Group, Dublin and the Centre for Science and Technology Studies (CWTS) The Netherlands.
7. Provided by Indecon International Economic Consultants, Dublin.

4 | ACHIEVEMENTS AND IMPACTS TO DATE

4.1 Introduction

Volume II provides details of the questions pursued by the visiting experts during their site visits to the institutions and a detailed account of their specific findings and conclusions. It also provides the results of the peer and bibliometric assessments, as well as summaries of the reports provided for the Committee by the independent consultants.

4.2 Value for Money

The overwhelming view of the visiting experts from outside Ireland is that the PRTLI investment is fully justified by the evidence of their site visits. However, the added value that has been achieved needs to be sustained with continued funding, if the value is to be maintained and increased.

The experts and the Committee are satisfied that PRTLI has significantly strengthened institutional research capacity and has enhanced the national and international competitiveness of its beneficiary institutions. It has provided the backbone which institutions have been able to use as leverage to acquire other research funding, notably from SFI and from the EU Framework Programme.

After PRTLI was established, several other initiatives were announced. These included SFI and the Research Councils. The leverage impacts of PRTLI on SFI have been very positive. A number of institutions reported to us that PRTLI had been a critical factor in successfully bidding for subsequent SFI funding. There is strong support in the institutions, which we fully endorse, for continuing to build on these complementarities, with PRTLI regularly providing the platform that enables institutions to successfully compete for a wide range of funding opportunities, nationally and internationally.

In many colleges the funding has totally transformed the environment for research and, in many cases, for teaching and learning too. Although the impact varies between institutions, the overall impact of PRTLI is hugely positive.

The main benefits are:

- Substantial enhancement of institutional capacity for world-class research, the enablement of a significant number of Irish researchers to participate in the international research community as scientific leaders and peers and the considerable strengthening of the '4th level' in Irish education.
- Significant increases in interdisciplinary research, in inter-institutional research collaborations and in joint research ventures between institutions.
- Retention and 'back-migration' of key researchers who otherwise would not have gone into research or would have done it abroad.

- Greatly increased ability of third level institutions to attract overseas talent (post docs etc), as well as encouraging the 'best' students to undertake Ph.D. programmes and to pursue careers in research in Irish institutions.

- Greatly enriched the educational environment for undergraduates and postgraduates.

- Greatly enhanced the ability of institutions to compete in a wider range of national and international funding programmes.

The range of indicator data developed for this assessment is perhaps not fully reflected in this Main Report, but is provided in total in Volume II. In summary, these data show provision for:

- 97,000 square metres of new research space, including almost 20,000 square metres of new library space.

- 5,800 new research spaces and 1,600 new library spaces for researchers.

- New capital equipment for advanced research to the value of €135 million, as well as €260 million for new research buildings.

- 34 senior researchers and professors (14 at professor level), 750 principal investigators, 450 postdoctoral appointments, almost 1,000 additional postgraduate posts for research and 70 research assistant posts.

- Facilities for 1,200 postgraduate students, funded from other sources and currently based in PRTLI centres.

- Production of 60 patent applications.

- Leverage of an additional €250 million for more than 1,000 new awards for research within PRTLI funded areas[8].

The overall impact of these developments has been to significantly increase the output of quality publications and international presentations, as well as the significant enhancement of the teaching and learning programmes of participating institutions. The headline indicators provided in Volume II show PRTLI investments have thus far produced:

- 4,600 scientific publications in the international literature, 620 books/chapters, more than 1,000 published contributions to scientific conferences, more than 2,000 presentations at international conferences and over 230 conferences hosted by Irish institutions.

- Creation of 22 new education programmes, 7 major new course modules and some 65 modifications to existing education programmes.

This enhancement of the research capabilities of the institutions has had a significant impact on their ability to win research grants and contracts. Compared to the pre-PRTLI period (1996/'97), the contract research budget of the institutions has increased markedly, in real terms. For example, the annual research grants and contracts income of University College Dublin has grown from €15 million to €33 million (+120%) and Trinity College Dublin from €17 million to €40 million (+135%) – excluding PRTLI grants.

Apart from volume impacts on research performance, we have also paid particular attention to the question of the international quality of PRTLI's research output and are quite reassured by the results to date. The impact of publications by PRTLI researchers in all fields is increasing and is in the category 'high to very high', according to the independent bibliometric analysis of a randomly selected sample of papers published by PRTLI researchers[9]. This evidence also shows that the impact of papers by PRTLI researchers is significantly higher than overall Irish impact scores. It is evident also that the quality of researchers attracted to work in PRTLI centres is high, as demonstrated by their high-impact publications in the period prior to coming to Ireland. These bibliometric results are corroborated by the outcome of the peer reviews of published PRTLI papers that was co-ordinated for us by independent consultants, CIRCA. Peers were of the view that PRTLI publications were of a high international standard and represent a major contribution to knowledge.

Given that PRTLI is still in the early stage of development and the relatively recent origins of these publications, we find the evidence of these analyses quite persuasive. We believe that that PRTLI is producing high quality research results of international interest.

4.3 Institutional Culture

PRTLI has made significant progress towards establishing the practice of strategic research planning in Irish third level institutions. We found plentiful evidence that institutions have been engaged in serious internal prioritisation. Where a strategic planning focus already existed, it can be credited with having greatly accelerated the process. We believe however, that there is still much to be done to fully embed these practices into institutional culture and we strongly support the retention of the emphasis on strategic planning in the PRTLI assessment criteria. Nonetheless, there is clear evidence that PRTLI has changed institutional thinking and has brought about an extraordinary transformation in the way third level institutions undertake research. In many cases, it has stimulated the introduction of processes and structures, while in others, it has enabled more effective implementation of strategies and plans. It is also bringing about a radical transformation in the environment for research in these institutions, as evidenced by the enthusiasm, energy and self-assurance that we encountered during our visits.

' 'S). Bibliometric study on research funded by the Higher Education Authority. April 2004.

It has induced both institutional and programmatic change through its fostering of a more effective institutional prioritisation process, allied to a more extensive examination of research strengths and weaknesses by the institutions themselves.

PRTLI has generally been beneficial in developing scale and critical mass in the institutions. Its emphasis on inter-institutional collaboration appears to have greatly assisted this objective and there are several remarkable examples of institutions together offering a scale of inter-institutional operations that heretofore would have been inconceivable. The Dublin Molecular Medicine project, involving three of the Dublin universities, is an outstanding example.

Neither the significance of these changes, nor their value to the Irish research enterprise should be underestimated. A wholly new collaborative culture, at all levels, is emerging as a result of PRTLI.

In addition to stimulating collaboration, PRTLI has also embedded a competitive ethos at institutional level. Individuals and centres now compete at institutional level for access to PRTLI. Institutions are making choices. Institutions have become more competitive and indicated to us that they welcome competitive funding opportunities – but insist that the size of the funding envelope must be maintained.

4.4 Teaching and Learning

Institutions in general saw PRTLI as having a positive impact on teaching and learning, although these impacts, as expected, are greater at the postgraduate levels than in the undergraduate domain. Teaching and learning impacts are evident in a wide range of new and varied undergraduate and graduate programmes.

In summary, the indicators attributable to PRTLI in respect of its impacts on the teaching and learning environment show:

* The creation of 22 new courses, the addition of 7 new modules to ongoing programmes and over 65 changes or modifications to existing courses.
* The accreditation and introduction (for the 22 new courses referred to above) of 7 new bachelor degree programmes, 2 post graduate diploma programmes, 11 new masters degree programmes and 2 new diploma programmes.

The visiting international experts were very positive about PRTLI's efforts to strengthen the interaction between teaching and research and found that the HEA insistence on a strong linkage between research and teaching was a unique and significant advantage of the PRTLI approach. While other research funding may be driven by narrower or more immediate industrial or sectoral needs, our view is that PRTLI lays deeper foundations. Its close links with the formation of human capital and education policy generally, as well as the importance of the teaching and learning criterion to its success, means that it has found an appropriate home within the jurisdiction of the Department of Education and Science.

The range of expertise that is now available in the PRTLI centres is much wider than in a traditional department. PRTLI has also attracted very high level expertise from home and abroad to these centres. According to the visiting experts, these advantages are available to students thanks to an evident open and enthusiastic ethos that pervades most of the new PRTLI centres. The experts found that relations between students and staff in most centres are very open and friendly. This is linked to increasingly multi- and inter-disciplinary research projects. Most centres provide internships or placements for undergraduates, giving them real experience of the application of research.

The state-of-the-art equipment and facilities provided by PRTLI that could not previously be afforded, are used for undergraduate as well as for postgraduate projects and for mainline research. The new buildings and facilities impress and attract students onto new courses run by the PRTLI centres.

Increased contact between undergraduates and PRTLI post docs was a benefit frequently mentioned by those interviewed, both in educational terms, and in encouraging participation in higher degrees. The contacts developed with undergraduates conducting fourth year projects appears to have been particularly effective and is crucial in developing '4th level' capacity. Undergraduates carry out fourth year projects working as a team alongside postgraduates and post docs. This provides expertise and experience for the students, and gives them confidence to continue to a postgraduate degree. It also acts as an informal conduit for career guidance. Undergraduates are generally required, or at least encouraged, to give research seminars, and are tutored in presentation skills. We believe that the educational environment under these conditions is extremely stimulating, effective and rather unique.

The development of new interdisciplinary and other courses and modules has benefited both undergraduate and postgraduate training. In some cases there have been inter-institutional linkages between colleges in Ireland and elsewhere, including Northern Ireland, with very positive effects. There is some evidence of institutions buying in new course modules from other colleges.

Many centres are making positive efforts to reach out to first and second level school children in order to stimulate an interest in science and technology in third level education. Current research projects are used as illustrations. This is a noteworthy and important effort with world-wide interest.

Smaller institutions, especially the institutes of technology, have used the research engagement supported by PRTLI to improve and to update their teaching programmes – a major justification for some research engagement by the institutes of technology.

All of these trends to multi-disciplinary, inter-institutional research activities, coupled with the obvious enthusiasm engendered in the centres by PRTLI, have given students a much wider educational environment in which to learn. The face of third level teaching and learning, as well as of research, has been altered hugely in Ireland.

4.5 Collaboration

The evidence on collaboration points to a new culture of multidimensional collaboration establishing itself in Irish research − collaboration between the academic departments of institutions, between the institutions themselves (including the institutes of technology) between scientific disciplines, between research and teaching and with international research groups. For example, at UCD, chemists now work with clinicians. The Conway Institute at UCD engages a total of 21 different departments in interdisciplinary research. Trinity College collaborates with UCD. Universities collaborate more closely with groups within institutes of technology. New interdisciplinary research clusters are emerging. For example, the Institute of Technology Sligo is leading a cluster that involves three universities, NUIG, UCC and UL. Almost 30% of the programmatic funding under PRTLI has gone to the collaborating partners in inter-institutional programmes. The research landscape is dramatically changing. PRTLI has also facilitated stronger and wider international collaborations at most institutions and it has enabled some to take leadership of international projects.

PRTLI has changed researcher attitudes about the value of interdisciplinarity and the institutional environment for it. Collaboration has helped to improve the scale of operations of many institutions and it has assisted institutions in accessing other funding sources. The headline indicators include:

- Establishment of 40 new inter-institutional research programmes, with 2,000 researchers directly involved and engaging third level institutions countrywide, including Northern Ireland universities.
- Creation of 7 new joint research facilities that are shared between two or more institutions.
- Engagement of 10 institutes of technology in formal research collaboration with the universities. Six of these research collaborations are led by an institute of technology.
- 100% increase in the number of collaborative agreements between institutions and a 70% increase in formal structures for management of inter-institutional collaboration, compared with the pre-PRTLI position.

We also heard evidence from industrial representatives of a strengthening of industrial collaboration with, and of interest in, PRTLI funded institutions, precisely because of the quality of the research capabilities that are now becoming available. PRTLI researchers have so far secured over €3 million directly from industrial partners for research activity in areas of PRTLI focus. Details of other industrial and commercial impacts are outlined in the report by the CIRCA consultants in Volume II.

4.6 Internationalisation impacts

The extensive and successful participation of Irish third level institutions in international research programmes, and especially in the EU Framework Programme, is a historical fact and is well documented. It is not evident to us that the availability of a strong domestic source of research funds, like PRTLI, has reduced the interest or enthusiasm of Irish researchers in any way towards participation in international programmes. On the contrary, some report that PRTLI has enabled stronger and successful EU bids, while others have specifically sought funds through PRTLI for increased EU collaboration. The bibliometric analysis of PRTLI publications shows that international collaboration is strong, with 30% of the research output that was examined involving collaboration with international partners. And it appears that the significant number of non-national researchers attracted by PRTLI funding has increased contacts with overseas research groups.

4.7 Humanities and Social Sciences

PRTLI has been designed to promote world-class research across all disciplines. There is evidence that it is succeeding in doing so for the Humanities and Social Sciences as well as for the Sciences and Engineering. PRTLI money has led to the opening of one world-class research library at TCD and another is planned for UCC. Several research centres in the Humanities and Social Sciences have been opened and the visiting experts and peer reviewers are clear that work of exceptional quality, much of it innovative and interdisciplinary, is coming out of these centres. Much of it will contribute to knowledge useful to Ireland's social and cultural development – examples here include PRTLI-funded projects on urban traffic management; on identity, diversity and citizenship; on how changing notions of identity and the function of public and private memory have helped to shape the politics and culture of modern Ireland; and on how processes of human settlement and historical change impact on the modern world. It is hoped that further rounds of PRTLI will continue to devote some money to the Humanities and Social Sciences and may be more welcoming to bids from those conducting research into the Performing and Creative Arts.

4.8 The Institutes of Technology

Impacts on the institutes of technology have varied. In total, 10 have participated, 6 as lead partners. While the teaching emphasis within the institutes has limited the impact of PRTLI compared with the universities, most readily acknowledge that PRTLI has been positive in bringing about a cultural change towards research at the institutes, stimulating greater prioritisation of institutional investment in research and in supporting and facilitating collaboration with other institutions, notably with the universities. We are conscious of the difficulties encountered by the institutes – infrastructural deficits, inadequate facilities and limited track records in leading edge research – in accessing PRTLI in competition with the much stronger universities. We are also aware of the institutes' criticisms of feedback from the assessment process, especially the written feedback, which is important to them in improving their future performance. Despite these difficulties, however, the institutes themselves acknowledge that participation in the PRTLI process has on the whole been positive for them. Our view is that the institutes should, indeed must, continue to compete for PRTLI funding as collaborators with the stronger universities and whenever they have the required strengths, as lead partners. We would not support, however, any dilution of the entry conditions to PRTLI in order to favour or facilitate the easier access of institutes of technology. We would be concerned that any move in this direction would reduce the competitive ethos of PRTLI, which we consider is critical in maintaining the high quality of funded proposals.

4.9 Management and Organisational change

PRTLI has coincided with and in some cases facilitated important changes in the management structures within its participating institutions, and has facilitated clearer responsibility and delegation. A typical reform has been the establishment of research offices and Deans/Vice Presidents for Research.

Some professionalisation of research management at the institutions is evident. This has included the establishment of professional managers, including Centre Directors, which has assisted in freeing up researchers from administrative tasks. There was evidence that where the leadership of centres was strong academically, but not strong managerially, changes to centre leadership had been made. Nettles have been grasped more firmly than in the past.

Headline indicators for research management at seven lead institutions show the extent of the improvements in place or in process, compared to pre-PRTLI times, in particular[10]:

- 7 institutions with a strategic planning process for research in operation, compared to 1 in 1995. All 12 of the institutions profiled for this study now have a long term strategic plan in place.
- 7 with a Research VP/Dean appointed compared to 2 in 1995
- 6 with a Research Committee in place compared to 4 in 1995
- 7 with arrangements for long and short term financial projections in place compared to 1 in 1995
- 7 with management information systems in place or being implemented compared to 3 in 1995.

In addition, of the 12 institutions with a strategic plan in place, all had undertaken at least one formal review of the plan since 2001.

PRTLI has generally impacted positively in terms of focusing the need for greater accountability within institutions. This has also fostered the introduction of new systems for financial management and management information systems.

Project directors have reported that all designated funding for successful bids is being allocated by the institution to these projects in accordance with the institution's agreement with the HEA. No specific difficulties were identified in this context.

---

10. These are the 7 institutions profiled in the 1996 CIRCA Report for the HEA.

Centres are generally positive about, or at least satisfied with, the HEA's management of the PRTLI. The reporting requirements are not regarded as being onerous, but could be simplified.

4.10 Innovation Impacts

At this early stage, it is difficult to say what the commercial impacts of PRTLI research will be or what impacts the programme will have on Ireland's innovation system. We note the evidence of patenting activity by PRTLI researchers, with 60 or so patent applications to date and we are aware from our discussions with industrial representatives that the quality of PRTLI facilities is already attracting industrial interest. We can say also that we sensed little or no reticence in the institutions on this issue[11]. On the contrary, institutional policies are generally supportive of technology transfer and commercialisation initiatives and a number of institutions have or are improving their support services and facilities in this area. University College Dublin, for example, now has a Vice President for Innovation and most colleges are attempting to improve awareness of IP through seminars and training programmes. Enterprise Ireland (EI) has recently introduced a number of initiatives to support commercialisation that will assist the third level sector and the Higher Education Authority has called for institutional strategies that will take specific account of commercialisation[12]. We note however, the criticisms of our visiting experts on the awareness of IP issues at the level of the individual researchers and it may be that while the institutions and the Government agencies are making an effort, it is not adequately resourced, by comparison with the scale of activity in European institutions, for example, and its penetration is still relatively weak, especially at bench level. While the improvements mentioned above are encouraging, it seems that there is still much to be done. These issues are discussed further in Section 7.3

4.11 Human Resource Impacts

An increase in research and teaching quality is a first step towards securing the human resources necessary for a knowledge and innovation based economy. In these terms, PRTLI, because of its insistence on substantive links into teaching and learning in participating institutions, is having a very positive impact, both in volume and in quality terms. We see this as a key feature of PRTLI, one that differentiates it from the more straightforward research funding schemes. We strongly support this characteristic and feel that PRTLI can seed the emergence of an internationally strong '4th level' in Irish education and contribute to the provision of high quality human resources for the economy, provided this criterion is maintained and that funding is continued.

In addition, we have learned that the institutions appear to be now attracting high quality researchers from other countries and to be retaining more of their own high flyers. PRTLI also appears to have coincided with an increasing trend towards retention of PhD students and post docs in Ireland. Traditionally, many of these would have left for further training abroad.

f the widening industrial connections of PRTLI.
EA) to the Enterprise Strategy Group (ESG). 2004.

PRTLI has improved the retention and 'back-migration' of key researchers, raised the number of non-national researchers in the Irish research system and increased contacts with overseas research groups. It has, for example, brought 146 new postdoctoral appointments and 196 new postgraduate studentships into the Irish research system from outside of Ireland.

We found no evidence of major institutional downsides or researcher de-motivation that could be attributed to PRTLI. Apart from some understandable frustration expressed by the institutes of technology, in the main, the impacts of PRTLI on human resources and especially on the development of a strong 4th level in Ireland have been beneficial.

5 | ASPECTS AND AREAS FOR FURTHER IMPROVEMENT

5.1 Sustainability of PRTLI Investments

The major concern at this juncture is about the sustainability of PRTLI funded centres. Lack of forward financial planning within certain centres was a concern to many of the visiting international experts. Several commented on the apparent naivete of centre managements as to the full costs of running their centres. Some centres anticipate further rounds of PRTLI funding and seem entirely dependent on such funding. These appear to have no plans for funding of their future growth, or even for maintenance of their existing facilities[13]. In the main, we were disappointed that the institutions were not addressing this issue more directly. Most appear to assume a continuation of public funding on a similar level.

In contrast, other centres have viewed PRTLI as a means to build their competence so that they can compete for funding from public and private sources. These centres, appropriately, look to a wide range of national and international public and industrial sources for funding. This planning for post-PRTLI growth is, in our view, both appropriate and very desirable.

Sustainability is also influenced by overhead provision, which, in our opinion, is totally inadequate. Currently, PRTLI provides 15%. Taking account of the evidence of recent studies on indirect costs carried out under the aegis of the HEA that we have been informed about, we would consider that a figure of about 45% of recurrent costs for laboratory based research would be more realistic[14]. Not surprisingly, therefore, overheads continue to be an ongoing problem for the institutions. In common with many countries, the research institutions in Ireland do not recover the full costs of contract or competitive research. PRTLI's 15% overhead provision means that other activities must subsidise PRTLI funded research and inevitably this results in some thinning out of these, notably teaching. Unless full overhead recovery is achieved, some level of cross subsidisation will continue to be the only alternative available to ensure the continued funding of PRTLI projects. In the long term this cannot continue.

Sustainability is also influenced by the approach taken by institutions to overhead allocation to the PRTLI centres. Policy in some colleges means that as little as 10% of overheads on their external funding would be returned to the centres. The visiting experts fully accept that the colleges themselves ought to receive a fair return on their inputs to these new centres, but are also convinced that this low level of overhead return will not allow centres to maintain their facilities.

We also note that capital cost inflation has adversely impacted on efficiency of infrastructure spend to-date and has forced institutions to divert resources from other activities to support the PRTLI centres.

---

13. It should be noted that some centres are in the early stages of their development and have not yet completed their buildings.
14. The Report of the Research Group on Research Overheads (July 2003) estimated the overhead recovery rates required for five third level institutions of between 35.1% to 57.5% of recurrent costs - pay and non-pay direct costs, excluding equipment - with an average of 45%.

5.2 Continuity and Stability of Research Funding

In our experience, continuity and stability of funding and the predictability of disbursements are essential in effectively managing the development of a sustainable research capability.

The general view across institutions is that considerable uncertainty surrounds the provision of funding for maintenance of infrastructure, upgrading of equipment and provision for researchers' salaries. These uncertainties have caused problems, both in morale and in recruitment of top-flight researchers. A Government commitment to sustained support for PRTLI over another planning period (of up to ten years) would do much to reassure the research community, nationally and internationally.

We have been told that the recent 'pause' in PRTLI funding has been damaging. It has undermined confidence, nationally and internationally, and has explicitly signalled a lack of commitment in public policy towards the research enterprise generally. It has undermined the capacity to attract other sources of funding. The testimony of stakeholders and of the representatives of industry on this point was consistently strong and insistent. But more importantly, the general view is that there is a need for provision of core recurrent funding to sustain the PRTLI centres.

The reductions in core grant funding to the universities that have been reported to us, make matters worse.

The timing of capital and current funding by PRTLI needs to be synchronised. The capital/current ratio was wrong during the earlier PRTLI Cycles. It was better later, but needs further improvement. There is a need for greater coordination between capital and recurrent funding.

Institutions are strongly of the view, which we fully support, that there is a need for greater coherence of research funding at Government level. A rapidly growing system that lacks coherence is bound to end up in disarray. The matter is therefore urgent. Solutions should not however involve additional layers of bureaucracy, or result in the concentration of research funding in a single agency or Government Department. Diversity is essential for a healthy funding system. A structure at the centre of Government is needed that will engage the main funding bodies in the co-ordination of funding policies across the board and ensure the maximum value added from the totality of Government support for the national research agenda.

5.3 Links to the Irish Innovation System

We believe that PRTLI will establish the foundations for knowledge intensive innovation in the Irish economy, which will ultimately bring positive results, provided the required complimentary measures to support all elements of the innovation complex are in place and working well together.

However, our discussions on the Irish innovation system have left us with a concern that the concept of a national innovation system, its distinctive operating characteristics in an Irish context, its constituent elements, their roles and interactions, appear not to be very clearly defined. We have to say that there seems to us to be little common agreement on how the national innovation system actually works in Ireland, or indeed of its requirements. Naturally, this lack of consensus increases the difficulties of an effective positioning of PRTLI with respect to its contribution to the innovation system. We believe that an examination of this issue, focusing particularly on the role and contribution of the research, education and training domain to the innovation system and the interlinked characteristics of these three elements within this domain, would be appropriate and timely.

We are aware from our interviews that the agencies responsible for industrial policy are concerned at what they perceive as a lack of an enterprise perspective in the PRTLI. We are confident however, that private sector 'pull' can be expected when the true potential of the capabilities being established in third level institutions is fully appreciated and we are aware that the quality of some PRTLI facilities is already attracting industrial interest. Specifically in this regard, we fully endorse the strategic dimension of PRTLI, primarily because it demands a careful assessment by the institutions of the external environment in which they operate, including consideration of the business and enterprise policy agenda and its needs. We would like to see a stronger consideration by the institutions themselves of this element of strategic planning in future and believe that it will help to more definitively position PRLTI and its contribution within the national innovation system.

A major concern of our visiting experts was the low level of appreciation of IP issues by individual researchers that were interviewed and the low level of exposure to formal training in IP management and protection. They report that IP management is often viewed by individual researchers as the responsibility of others in the college, mainly the technology transfer and commercialisation wing of the institution. In other words, the issue of IP protection and management was, in many centres, regarded as a responsibility of the wider college, rather than as a core need of the centre itself and its researchers. We are aware that many institutions have made improvements in this area in recent times, however, we have heard of serious under-resourcing, in comparison to similar institutions internationally, and we have the view that the penetration of current awareness efforts needs to be improved. Awareness of the principles of IPR is a fundamental need for R&D professionals. While many institutions offer such training, the experience of the visiting experts is that a high proportion of PRTLI researchers appear to have had no training at all on this issue.

Whereas most of the institutions have IP management staff, who are available to assist the PRTLI centres, the centres themselves must ensure that their individual researchers and students are familiar with the principles of IPR. The perception that IP protection is necessarily adverse to the need to publish would appear also to remain within some centres.

At national level, the recent launch of a voluntary National Code of Practice on IP by the Irish Council for Science, Technology and Innovation (ICSTI) is a welcome development. Hopefully, this will help a wider awareness of the issues involved. However, in addressing the criticisms of our visiting experts, we suggest that consideration might be given to the establishment of a centralised arrangement that would provide advice and guidance, specialist support and training, as well as monitoring, to the institutions in this area.

All centres had developed initiatives to communicate their findings and/or developments to potential users and these are generally appropriate in their intent. However, the scale and quality of the specific activities was highly variable and many centres have not adequately developed these mechanisms.

At this point, an intensive discussion between industry and academia should be initiated and strengthened in order to identify suitable fora for discussion and for concrete collaboration. An Irish consensus on public/private co-operation should be identified and clear legal framework for intellectual property rights constructed.

5.4 Human Resources for Research

PRTLI has greatly increased the number of post-doctoral fellows engaged in basic research in Ireland and this must be welcomed. Some of these, especially in science and engineering, are now being recruited into the private sector within Ireland. More can and should be done to plan a career structure for these highly-skilled products of the new environment. This will be particularly important in maintaining incentives for staff and attracting leading researchers. However, success in this area has varied across institutions. Development of a career structure for post-doctoral fellows is a requirement for a viable research infrastructure and needs the urgent attention of the HEA and of the Department of Education and Science.

5.5 Teaching and Learning

We found impressive evidence that PRTLI has resulted in many new courses and programmes for students. Our experts have reported a very positive student response to the closer proximity and improved access that they now have to research expertise and it is evident that the educational environment for students has improved.

On the whole, there is clear evidence that PRTLI has had a positive impact on teaching and learning. While we welcome these improvements, we would like to see more attention given to instruction, as opposed to the quantity and diversity of programmes on offer. With further effort, PRTLI can help to stimulate new and innovative teaching methods/instruction tools, innovative learning environments, more innovative linkages and new binding mechanisms at the research and teaching interface.

We are also aware from our visits to colleges that there is evidence, in some instances, of an emerging tension between teaching & learning objectives and research objectives of the institutions. A teaching and learning overload may be occurring elsewhere in these institutions as a consequence of the institutional commitment to PRTLI research. In some cases too, there appears to be a need to divert additional institutional resources in order to meet the growing needs of PRTLI centres. At the level of the institution, these tensions, unless addressed, will ultimately be dysfunctional and damaging to the overall strategy of the institutions.

Research seminars are important mechanisms for communicating research developments and other new information to students at all levels. While such seminars are a feature of most centres, efforts to promote these events to undergraduates (and on occasion to post graduates) could be improved.

5.6 Collaboration

While much has been achieved in this respect, there is more to be done. As might be expected, a small number of centres had not achieved real interaction between the different disciplines and departments involved. The specific reasons for this were difficult to determine, but both HEA and the colleges should look more specifically at these centres to assess what steps might be taken to achieve the planned level of collaboration.

In some cases, there is evidence that collaboration has been tactical or funding driven, rather than strategic in nature. Collaboration will be more successful if it grows organically between mutual research interests, rather than being legislated or imposed. The main point is that collaboration must not be "legislated". In future, collaboration "as a path towards scale" or a method of building critical mass, would be the proper approach.

With some exceptions, the general view is that international collaboration in the EU Framework Programme has become very challenging.

The institutes of technology are very supportive of the collaborative ethos of PRTLI, but see scope for much greater exploitation of this dimension to their advantage.

The extent of industry collaboration, which is significant in some institutions, is growing. Volume II provides details.

5.7 Cultural Changes

While the cultural shift that has occurred in research planning and management in the institutions is evident and real, it is still early days and there is considerable working out and embedding of the new culture to be achieved by the institutions. We believe that they will need a continuation and reinforcement of PRTLI's strategic regime, if durable and longstanding improvements are to be achieved. In our opinion, there should be no relaxing of this central and unique feature of PRTLI.

In addition, within a strategic planning framework, there is a need to strengthen business and financial planning for all of the newly established research centres.

5.8 Linkages with the R&D System

A more explicit and better organised collaboration between PRTLI and SFI would be to the mutual benefit of both programmes and add value. We understand, for example, that up to 50% of SFI funded investigators are based at PRTLI Centres. There is an obvious synergy in this relationship, but it appears to us to be relatively unplanned. More explicit collaboration is needed between both, if this synergy is to be better and more fully exploited. Our view is that PRTLI provides the backbone and the deeper foundation on which specific initiatives like SFI depend and can build on, and without which, they cannot be fully effective. PRTLI is necessary to enable other initiatives to flourish. PRTLI ought to provide the platform for more focussed initiatives like SFI or the sectoral research needs of government departments.

5.9 Research Management

There is little experience in Ireland in managing research at the scale made possible by PRTLI and SFI funding. This has been highlighted in other reports[15]. This is most evident in some centres in relation to the administrative systems established, to financial planning and to equipment and facility maintenance arrangements. There is an under-provision of training for the management of new centres. Development of liaison between managers would also be useful in exchanging information and in exploring good management practices.

There are very different types of structures, reporting processes and status of centres within the universities. While this is not necessarily a problem, there is no sharing of management practice or operational information between centres.

A key challenge for the future development of institutions will be the management of relationships between faculties, departments and emerging PRTLI centres. A difficulty in this regard concerns the division of resources between faculties/departments and PRTLI centres and the balancing of research with teaching and learning objectives. The relationship between the new centres and the departmental backbone of the host institution is not a settled one. Mostly, this is seen as a partnership – "flexible interaction"- but tension exists. There is a lack of so-called "joined up thinking" at some institutions at top level in regard to the working out of this relationship. Some PRTLI centres complain about departmental restrictions on centre recruitment, for example, especially on senior appointments, contrary to stated priorities.

---

15. e.g. Baseline Assessment of Public Research System in Ireland in Biotechnology & ICT. Forfás 2002.

Several of the issues which arose hinge on the perception by the host college of the role of a PRTLI centre; and on the system of reporting and representation used. In some colleges the Centre Director and/or advisory panels of one form or another clearly have a strong role in decision-making on future research directions, and other centre issues. In a small number, the centre leadership appears to be temporary, and/or the centre is little more than a space within which the constituent departments perform research. However, the Committee is satisfied that where there had been problems of this kind, they have been or were being grasped.

Also, there is a need for better campus management and systems, including facilities management. For example, few institutions appear to have the data necessary to estimate the full costs of research, not to mention the overhead costs. The ability of institutions to efficiently respond to requests for greater transparency in accounting and costing will be influential in how well institutions are perceived by government and by the general public.

5.10 Management by HEA

The PRTLI process is generally perceived as satisfactory – "unusual by international standards, but a very fair process". Its integrity is widely respected by the institutions and the independence of the international assessment panel in project selection is, in our view, one of its outstanding strengths. We commend the Authority and its executive for their non-interventionist approach and for the establishment of a truly competitive process, committed to excellence in research.

We favour the retention of the unique institutional and strategic focus of PRTLI and would like to see more explicit consideration by the institutions of the industrial policy agenda and its priorities in framing their research strategies. This would help greatly to more firmly position PRTLI within the national system of innovation and would make its interaction with other non-education sector funding sources more explicit, thereby improving the coherence of overall funding arrangements.

We have considered the impacts of PRTLI in the context of the Government's spatial strategy, but we are firmly of the view that excellence and the strategic significance of the research itself must remain the overwhelming criteria in the PRTLI selection process.

There are a few areas for attention by the HEA. There is a need to improve the quality and extent of feedback to the institutions, as well as the feedback process. Institutions state that unsuccessful applicants have not been assisted by feedback on the strengths and weaknesses of their proposals.

There was a very consistent complaint about the inadequate feedback to centres from the 6-monthly reports to HEA.

Institutions would welcome opportunities to present proposals to adjudication panels and to be interviewed by panel members. Site visits by panel members would also be welcomed.

Some centres also noted the lack of visits by HEA staff. There are opportunities for the HEA executive to be more visible on campus in meeting and maintaining contacts with Heads of Centres and Principal Investigators.

6 | RECOMMENDATIONS

6.1 Introduction

Our main recommendations are directed at Government, the institutions and the HEA.

6.2 Recommendations for Government

- We are convinced that PRTLI has made significant progress in respect of all its objectives; progress that will ultimately manifest itself in stronger and better managed institutions, in centres of excellence that will be capable of matching the best internationally and in the formation of the highest quality human capital for the growing Irish economy. Fulfilment of this promise will require sustained Government investment over the long term. The full achievement of the high promise of PRTLI that we have found will depend on continuity of Government support and funding for this initiative. ***We strongly recommend consistent and sustained investment in this Programme by the Irish Government over the period of the current National Plan and its continuation for a further planning period of at least ten years.***

- In general, institutional strategy should be to continue to focus on the development of existing broad areas of comparative research strength. However, institutions are of the view, which we fully support, that it is important to be able to respond to new developments in the external environment, which demand flexibility and which may motivate adjustments of focus within broad areas of expertise. Building a strong research backbone, with a flexible response capability, is seen as a key objective of PRTLI. We believe that the Irish Government should avoid any narrowing of focus or overspecialisation in research carried out in third level institutions. ***We recommend that the Government continue to support a flexible and diverse funding system for third level institutions in Ireland; a system that underpins the highest quality teaching and learning in the institutions and that motivates and enables multiple research opportunities and potentials.*** We are convinced that this is the most effective way for an economy like Ireland's to further enhance its human capital and develop a robust '4th level' that will underpin its competitiveness in the globalising world economy.

- In proposing the above, we are conscious of a lack of coherence at national level in research funding arrangements. Ireland, like other countries, has a variety of research funding agencies, each with a specific mandate that is well embedded within the mission of the host Department and that supports sectoral policies for education, industry, health, agriculture, marine, environment etc. In this context, we note and support the search for better co-ordination mechanisms at national level that is currently underway. Whatever formula emerges from this, we believe that the alliance between research and sectoral policy is important and ought to be preserved. In regard to the two major players among these funding agencies, we are aware that the established demarcation between SFI and PRTLI appears to be breaking down. In particular, we would like to see more coherence between the funding decisions of PRTLI and SFI. We believe that this is possible and will be to the benefit of both initiatives and of the participating institutions. ***We recommend the establishment of the necessary arrangements to bring about improved coherence in research funding. We favour the establishment of a supervisory body at the highest*** *level (Taoiseach's Department) with participation of the funding agencies and with the aims of ensuring coherence and of retaining diversity in funding policies and programmes. It should be independently chaired, ideally by the Taoiseach and not by a sectoral minister. A transversal committee, chaired at the highest level, will help to produce the necessary coherence in funding, as good practice in other countries demonstrates. However, these arrangements should be administratively thin and flexible and avoid any heavy bureaucracy.*

- *Fundamentally, however, we recommend and emphasise the critical need for continuation of PRTLI funding for a considerable period into the future, if the progress in hand is to be consolidated.* And unanimously, we deplore the 'pause' in funding that occurred in 2003 and that happily is now rectified. We would fear for the durability of the entire edifice were such discontinuities to become a feature of government research funding policies in the future.

6.3 Recommendations for the Institutions

- All PRTLI centres need to undertake some basic business planning, which would take into account the funds required and the most likely sources of these, going forward. This would also include consideration of what actions are needed in the future to strengthen the prospects that centres will be successful in bidding for such funds. *We recommend the introduction of business planning for all newly established PRTLI centres and its requirement for all future funding applications under PRTLI.*

- There is likely to be a continued drive in many institutions to exploit potential commercialisation of research. To-date, while some institutions have developed commercialisation and IPR strategies, and some have even registered patents, much remains to be done in taking forward the commercially oriented research possibilities that will be generated under PRTLI. *In general, the colleges must pay greater attention to the commercial and business potential of investments made under the PRTLI. We recommend that the IPR arrangements in all colleges be strengthened and better resourced by the colleges themselves.*

- There are a number of management issues that need to be addressed. The most important of these is the need to define more precisely how the relationship between the traditional departmental and faculty structures of the colleges and their new research centres will be developed. We are concerned that this question may have been allowed to drift in some colleges in the expectation that practical experience will ultimately determine how matters will evolve. We do not support this approach. *We recommend that all colleges in receipt of PRTLI funding for centres should now specifically define the responsibility, authority and accountability parameters that will determine the desired relationship between these centres and the traditional college structures.*

- *Also, in relation to management, we recommend more management training for centre managers and opportunities for managers at different colleges to exchange information about effective management practices.*

- *We also recommend regular review of strategic planning at the institutions in order to assist the further focusing of activities in areas of strength and /or important emergent fields of research.*

- We have seen convincing evidence of the beneficial impacts of PRTLI on the institutes of technology, especially through their direct participation as programme leaders and also through collaborative arrangements with the universities. The pan-institutional networks that are now emerging and the mobility of personnel between institutions that is developing will accommodate the growth of new talent and will strengthen the whole research system at third level. While we acknowledge the severity of the competition that the institutes face in accessing PRTLI, we are against any relaxation of this competitive ethos, believing that it is the best way to ensure quality. *Therefore, while we strongly encourage the institutes of technology to continue their participation in PRTLI, we recommend against any relaxation of institutional competition or any ringfencing arrangements that would preferentially favour institute of technology participation.*

6.4 Recommendations for the HEA

- It will be necessary to strike a balance between adding new infrastructure and the ongoing requirement to maintain existing space and upgrade equipment. *In this context, our recommendation is that there should be a greater focus on people and equipment in the next round of PRTLI funding and rather less than heretofore on buildings – though some institutions still struggle with large infrastructural deficits.*

- Support for the continued development of earlier PRTLI investments should be performance based. *We recommend that only those centres meeting demanding performance criteria, to be specified and monitored by the HEA, should be eligible for further PRTLI funding.*

- We consider that more attention must be given to consideration of how PRTLI connects with the national system of innovation in Ireland and to ways of improving this link. *We recommend that HEA undertakes a specific study of the innovation system, from the perspective of research and education, to determine how best to improve the connections between PRTLI and the economic and industrial agendas of the relevant Government Departments and agencies.*

- In regard to the PRTLI process, *we recommend that the HEA –*
  - *improves the feedback process and the content of information provided to applicant institutions,*
  - *considers the introduction of vivas or other face to face opportunities for applicants to present proposals to assessors,*

- establishes a consistent set of indicators that will be used for programme monitoring. The indicators developed for this study may provide a basis for this.

- We believe that the inter-institutional collaboration ethos that is emerging in research can be transferred also to teaching. We found some evidence that institutions were willing to consider outsourcing or buying in specified course modules. ***We recommend that HEA undertakes a study of the opportunities for inter-institutional education programmes.***

- PRTLI has a visibility problem. The programme is not well known or appreciated outside of the education sector. It is hardly recognised at all in industry. The title itself is cumbersome and even participants admit to difficulties with it. ***We recommend that the public relations side of the Programme be considerably strengthened and possibly, HEA ought to consider a change of name or logo for the Programme.***

- *In recognition of the interim nature of this report, we recommend that HEA undertake a further assessment of PRTLI in 3 to 5 years time, including bibliometric assessments and building on the data assembled for this study.*

7 | APPENDICES

Appendix A. Abbreviations & Acronyms Used

AIT	Athlone Institute of Technology		HERD	Higher Education Expenditure on Research and Development
BCRI	Boole Centre for Research in Informatics (UCC)		HII	Humanities Institute of Ireland (UCD)
BSI	BioSciences Institute (UCC)		HRB	Health Research Board
BSN	Biopharmaceutical Sciences Network (RCSI)		H&SS	Humanities and Social Sciences
CAO	Central Applications Office		IAMS	Institute for Advanced Materials Science (TCD)
CI	Citation Index		IBEC	Irish Business and Employers Federation
CISC	Centre for Innovation & Structural Change (NUIG)		IBIA	Irish Bioindustry Association
CISS	Centre for Irish Scottish Studies (TCD)		IBS	Institute for Biopharmaceutical Sciences (RCSI)
CIT	Cork Institute of Technology		ICT	Information and Communication Technology
CMNES	Centre for Mediterranean and Near East Studies (TCD)		ICSTI	Irish Council for Science Technology & Innovation
COFORD	National Council for Forest Research and Development		IDA	Industrial Development Authority
CPP/FCMm	Number of Citations Per Publication/mean Field Citation Score		IITAC	Institute for Information Technology & Advanced Computational Research (TCD)
CSCB	Centre for Synthesis & Chemical Biology (UCD)		IIIS	Institute for International Integration Studies (TCD)
CSET	Centre for Science, Engineering and Technology (SFI Programme)		IIM	Institute of Immunology (NUIM)
CSHSHC	Centre for the Study of Human Settlement and Historical Change (NUIG)		IP	Intellectual Property
			IPCMF	Irish Pharmaceutical and Chemical Manufacturers Federation
CWTS	Centre for Science and Technology Studies, Leiden University		IPR	Intellectual Property Rights
DCU	Dublin City University		IRCHSS	Irish Research Council for the Humanities & Social Sciences
DES	Department of Education and Science		IRCSET	Irish Research Council for Science Engineering & Technology
DG Research	Directorate-General Research		ISSC	Institute for the Study of Social Change (UCD)
DIAS	Dublin Institute of Advanced Studies		IT	Institute of Technology or Information Technology
DIT	Dublin Institute of Technology			
DMMC	Dublin Molecular Medicine Centre		IT Carlow	Institute of Technology, Carlow
ECI	Environmental Change Institute (NUIG)		IT Sligo	Institute of Technology, Sligo
EI	Enterprise Ireland		LIT	Limerick Institue of Technology
ERI	Environmental Research Institute (UCC)		Met Eireann	The Irish Meteorological Service
ERTDI	Environment Research, Technological Development & Innovation measure		MIC	Mary Immaculate College, Limerick
			MIS	Management Information Systems
EPA	Environmental Protection Agency		MRI	Martin Ryan Institute
ESRI	Economic & Social Research Institute		MSSI	Materials and Surface Science Institute (UL)
EU	European Union		M-Zones	Smart Space Management (WIT)
EU FP	European Union Framework Programme		NCBES	National Centre for BioMedical Engineering Science (NUIG)
FP6	Sixth EU Framework Programme		NCC	National Competitiveness Council
F & HP	Food and Health Programme (UCC)		NCPST	National Centre for Plasma Science & Technology(DCU)
FOCAS	Facility for Optical Characterization and Spectroscopy (DIT)		NCSR	National Centre for Sensors Research (DCU)
FIRM	Food Institutional Research Measure		NDP	National Development Plan
FTE	Full-Time Equivalent		NICB	National Institute for Cellular Biotechnology (DCU)
GIS	Geographic Information System			
GMIT	Galway Mayo Institute of Technology		NIH	National Institutes of Health (USA)
HEA	Higher Education Authority		NIRSA	National Institute for Regional and Spatial Analysis (NUIM)
HEAnet	Provider of broadband internet services to Irelands third level institutions			

NMRC	National Microelectronics Research Centre (UCC)
NNF	National Nanofabrication Facility (UCC)
NUI	National University of Ireland
NUIG	National University of Ireland, Galway
NUIM	National University of Ireland, Maynooth
OECD	Organisation for Economic Co-operation and Development
PD	Post doctoral fellow
PG	Post graduate student
Ph.D.	Doctor of Philosophy
PHG	Programme for Human Genomics (RCSI)
PI	Principal Investigator
PRTLI	Programme for Research in Third Level Institutions
RA	Research Assistant
R & D	Research and Development
RCSI	Royal College of Surgeons in Ireland
RINCE	Research Institute for Networks and Communications Engineering (DCU)
RTD	Research and Technical Development
RTDI	Research Technology, Development and Innovation
RTI	Research, Technology and Innovation
SC	Steering Committee
SFI	Science Foundation Ireland
SPD	St. Patrick's College, Drumcondra
STRIDE	Forestry Sub-Programme
Teagasc	Irish Agriculture and Food Development Authority
T&L	Teaching and Learning
TCD	Trinity College Dublin
TRIP	Centre for Transportation Research and Innovation
UCC	University College Cork
UG	Under-Graduate Student
UCD	University College Dublin
UII	Urban Institute of Ireland (UCD)
UL	University of Limerick
WIT	Waterford Institute of Technology

Countries:
Austria AT, Belgium BE, Czech Republic CZ, Cyprus CY;
Denmark DK, Estonia EE, Finland FI, France FR, Germany DE,
Greece GR, Hungary HU, Iceland IS, Ireland IE, Italy IT,
Japan JP, Latvia LV, Lithuania LT, Luxembourg LU, Malta MT,
Netherlands NL, Norway NO, Poland PL, Portugal PT,
Slovakia SK, Slovenia SI, Spain ES, Sweden SE, Switzerland CH,
Turkey TR, United Kingdom UK, United States of America US.

The Proposed Assessment

It is now proposed to undertake a comprehensive assessment of the progress, results and achievements of PRTLI to date.

The period for this will be from the commencement of PRTLI in 1998 to July 2003. Both completed projects and more recently funded projects will be included in the assessment.

The objectives of the assessment are to monitor the operation of the PRTLI programmes and to inform future research policy:

Monitoring of programme:

- Assess the progress, performance and achievements of PRTLI programmes funded to date and whether these are on track towards their stated longer-term goals,
- Ascertain the extent to which the specific aims and objectives of PRTLI in respect of strategic planning, interinstitutional collaboration, quality research and teaching impacts are being met,
- Examine the adherence to documented plans, budgets, methodologies and standards,
- Assess the administration of the programme by the HEA executive.

Policy Review:

Address broader research policy and funding issues, the strategic positioning of PRLTI in relation to other funding programmes currently available and including the role of PRTLI in the funding of research core capacity and capital funding.

Make recommendations for the future development of PRTLI.

The key questions that the assessment will be expected to address are:

- Has PRTLI helped to enhance the international research reputation of the participating institutions?
- Has PRTLI been a catalyst for change in the management, planning and social environment within and between institutions in the research system? Has PRTLI resulted in the empowerment of Deans of Research, Centre Directors and other senior research staff within the institutions?
- Has PRTLI helped to improve the quality of curriculum, course provision and instruction at the institution and is it helping to improve the quality of graduate output?
- Has PRTLI encouraged co-operation between researchers by promoting and embedding inter-institutional collaboration between third level institutions in order to counterbalance limitations of scale in individual institutions and to strengthen research outputs?
- Have any commercial potentialities, IPR, start-up and technology transfer, investment opportunities or other social, economic or development potentials been created by PRTLI?
- Where does PRTLI fit within national research funding policy going forward?

The assessment will be undertaken by a high level international Assessment Committee, chaired by an experienced individual of high international reputation. There will be three other members, all with international scholarly and research reputations. An independent Secretary to the Assessment Committee will be appointed to support the Committee directly for the duration of the Assessment.

The Assessment Committee will advise on assessment methods and procedures, monitor and assess the work of research and teaching/learning experts and independent consultants. The committee will also undertake site visits to participating institutions, as needed, and prepare a final report for the HEA.

The Secretary, independent consultants and the HEA Executive will provide support to the Assessment Committee as required.

Structure of the Assessment Process

The methodology is structured around the three selection criteria for PRTLI and will comprise five interconnected modules.

Module 1 – Institutional Strategy and Management Impacts

The Assessment Committee will itself take responsibility for the assessment of PRTLI impacts on the institutional context and environment for research, particularly strategic planning and management and interinstitutional collaboration. This will be carried out through site visits and interviews with the Presidents of the institutions and the Vice Presidents/Deans of Research. This will also include institutions that were unsuccessful in applications for PRTLI funding.

Interview formats and outline questionnaires for these discussions will be developed by the HEA Executive.[a] Presidents will be invited to provide an advance statement on PRTLI impacts at their institutions.

The Committee will also assess the management of the Programme by HEA.

Module 2 – Research Quality Assessment

The impact of PRTLI on research quality in the institutions will be assessed through a combination of:
site visits to selected institutions/programmes and discussions with researchers by selected specialists,
desk-based peer assessments of a sample of PRTLI supported research publications,
bibliometric analysis of a sample of PRTLI publications output, prior to and since PRTLI funding

The site visits will review the progress and performance of the research based on discussions and presentations by PRTLI funded researchers. The quality and relevance of research facilities and infrastructure provided by PRTLI and the effective utilisation of these will be reviewed, as well as the adherence by the research team(s) to commitments given in the funded proposal.

---

a. This work was conducted by the independent consultants and approved by the International Assessment Committee.

Specialists will be selected for these visits, with the assistance of the Assessment Committee and they will report to the Assessment Committee. Assessment Committee members may also participate in these site visits, if desired.

For the peer-based assessments of PRTLI publications, a selection of publications nominated by PRTLI Principal Investigators will be made. Peers will be asked to assess the research results reported in these papers in terms of the quality of research methods employed and the international significance and standing of the results obtained.

The bibliometric element of this module will be based on a citation analysis of selected PRTLI investigators prior to and since receipt of PRTLI support. An independent group will be commissioned to carry out this study.

A draft synthesis report on research quality, based on the results of these investigations, will be prepared for consideration by the Assessment Committee.

Module 3 – Teaching and Learning Impacts

The teaching and learning impacts of PRTLI will be assessed by selected experts in teaching and learning, based on site visits and interviews with the relevant Registrars, Deans, Department Heads, Teaching and Learning Departments and students at the institutions.

The effectiveness of the specific measures and structures that have been put in place to ensure the linkage between PRTLI funded research and the teaching and learning programmes of the institution, will be reviewed.

Interview formats and draft questionnaires will be developed.
A draft synthesis report, based on the results of these investigations, will be prepared for consideration by the Assessment Committee.

Module 4 – Thematic Studies

Two cross-cutting thematic studies will be subcontracted to external consultants:

• Collaboration impacts

The assessment will seek to establish the quality, value-added, management effectiveness and sustainability of PRTLI supported collaborations between third level institutions, based on a review of relevant documentation and site visits to a selection of collaborating institutions.

Detailed terms of reference will be prepared for the consultants, who will report to the Assessment Committee.

- Policy relevance and coherence

The assessment will review and assess the relevance and validity of the stated objectives of PRTLI against the background of current and anticipated developments in research funding and the positioning of PRTLI in the context of other research funding programmes at national level. The consultants will interview key PRTLI stakeholders (including private donors, opinion leaders) and representatives of relevant government departments and research funding bodies and will report to the Assessment Committee.

Detailed terms of reference will be prepared for the consultants.

Module 5 – Assessment Metrics and Indicators

The HEA executive, in consultation with the Assessment Committee, will assemble programme metrics and indicators to provide a quantitative and qualitative framework for the work of the Committee, experts and consultants. While a necessary, but not a sufficient requirement for the assessment of a programme of this nature, they will provide a reference point and support for the deliberations of the Assessment Committee.

The quantitative indicators to be assembled will include:

Input indicators

Detailed financial profiles of PRTLI allocations to institutions, programmes, disciplines and facilities etc will be developed.

Output indicators

Quantitative indicators to measure programme outputs will include the following:

- sq. metres of new/renovated laboratory, library and office space
- number of new post graduates, post doctorates and faculty employed
- numbers of research publications, including bibliometric analysis of selected PRTLI funded PIs, before and after PRTLI support
- numbers of new/modified teaching courses and programmes provided with PRTLI inputs
- management indicators; strategic plans/new structures/new posts, including benchmarking with 1996 CIRCA Group Report
- interinstitutional collaborative agreements/structures/joint publications

Impact indicators

Whilst PRTLI was launched in 1998, allocations first reached the colleges in 1999. Thus whilst most PRTLI investments have yet to reach maturity, with some allocations being made as recently as late 2001, the assessment will document the evidence available to show PRTLI impacts on:
- the international research reputations of the participating institutions
- the emergence of centres of research excellence of significant critical mass within the research system

- research planning and management processes and the research environment at and between the institutions in the third level research system
- the quality of teaching and learning programmes and improvements in the quality of graduate output
- the existence of new structures and processes which ensure research/teaching linkages
- the generation of commercial potentialities
- the contribution to national research policy

Indicative Timeframe for the Assessment

It is envisaged that the assessment will be initiated in September, with site visits taking place in October/November, 2003. All reports from different modules will be reviewed and compiled by the Assessment Committee and it is envisaged that the report will be published by end of Q2 2004

Appendix C. Visiting Experts & Peer Reviewers

Shading indicates that the Expert Peer carried out site visits to a number of PRTLI-funded centres

Name	Affiliation
Prof John Baines	Oriental Institute, University of Oxford, UK.
Prof Ken Barbarick	Department of Soil and Crop Sciences, Colorado State University, USA.
Prof Chris Bobonich	Department of Philosophy, Stanford University, USA.
Prof Adrian Bone	Head of Research, School of Pharmacy & Biomolecular Sciences, University of Brighton, UK.
Prof Guenther Bonn	Head of the Institute of Analytical Chemistry, University of Innsbruck, Austria.
Prof Michael Braddick	Department of History, University of Sheffield, UK.
Prof Shaun Brennecke	Head of Department, Obstetrics and Gynaecology, The Royal Women's Hospital, Victoria, Australia.
Prof John Bryden	Director, Arkleton Centre for Rural Development Research, Aberdeen University, UK.
Dr Caroline Bucklow	CEO, Institute of Learning and Teaching in Higher Education, York, UK.
Prof David Butler	Department of Civil and Environmental Engineering, Imperial College, London, UK.
Prof Reg Byron	School of Social Sciences and International Development, University of Wales, Swansea, UK.
Prof Christopher Coggins	WAMTECH, Luton, UK.
Prof Malcolm Cresser	Head of Environment Department, University of York, UK.
Prof Vanetta d'Andrea	Director, Higher Education Development Centre, City University, London, UK.
Prof Roy (E.R.) Davies	Head, Machine Vision Group, Department of Physics, University of London, UK.
Prof Bill Dawson	Visiting Professor at Sheffield University, UK. Formerly Head of Research with Eli Lily UK.
Prof Gerard Delanty	Head of Department of Sociology, Social Policy and Social Work Studies, University of Liverpool, UK.
Prof Ian Diamond	CEO, Economic and Social Research Council, UK.
Prof Gordon Dougan	Department of Biological Sciences, Imperial College, London, UK.
Dr Richard Dyer	Director, Babraham Institute, Cambridge, UK.
Prof Marianne Elliot	OBE, Professor of Modern History and Director of the Institute for Irish Studies, University of Liverpool, UK.
Prof Geoffrey Evans	Official Fellow, Nuffield College, University of Oxford, UK.
Prof Sue Fairweather-Tait	Head of Nutrition Division, Institute of Food Research, Norwich Research Park, UK.
Prof Garret Fitzgerald	Chair, Dept of Pharmacology, Director, Centre for Experimental Therapeutics, University of Pennsylvania, USA.
Dr Stephen J. Fonash	Director, Nanofabrication Facility, Pennsylvania State University, USA.
Prof Laszlo Forro	Director, Institute of the Physics of Complex Matter, École Polytechnique Federale de Lausanne, Switzerland.
Prof Jean-Pierre Fouassier	Department of General Photochemistry, École National de Chemie de Mulhouse, France.
Prof Robert M. Fowler	Department of Religion, Baldwin-Wallace College, Ohio, USA.
Prof Jiali Gao	Department of Chemistry, University of Minnesota, USA.
Prof Jonathan Gershuny	Director, Institute for Social and Economic Research, Essex University, UK.
Prof Martin Goodman	Wolfson College and Oriental Institute, University of Oxford, UK.
Prof Peter A. Hall	Department of Pathology, Queen's University, Belfast, Northern Ireland.

Name	Affiliation
Prof Eric Hall	Professor of Radiation Oncology and Radiology, Director, Centre for Radiological Research, College of Physicians & Surgeons, Columbia University, New York, USA.
Prof Ian Halliday	CEO, Particle Physics and Astronomy Research Council, UK.
Prof Mark Hanson	Director, Centre for Fetal Origins of Adult Disease, Princess Anne Hospital, Southampton, UK.
Prof Anthony Harriman	Professor of Physical Chemistry and Co-Director of the Molecular Photonics Laboratory, Department of Chemistry, University of Newcastle upon Tyne, UK.
Prof Frank E. Harris	Quantum Theory Project, University of Florida, USA.
Prof Mick Healy	Director, Geography Management Research Unit, University of Gloucestershire, UK.
Dr Lois Hetland	Principle Investigator in Teaching and Learning, Harvard Graduate School of Education, MA, USA.
Prof Seamus Higson	Institute of Bioscience, Cranfield University, UK.
Prof Alan Jenkins	Oxford Centre for Staff and Learning and Development, Oxford Brookes University, UK.
Prof Jeff Kenworthy	Institute for Sustainable Settlements and Technology Policy, Murdoch University, Western Australia.
Prof Ullrich Kockel	Director, Centre for European Studies, University of the West of England, UK.
Prof Kurt Komarek	Austrian Academy of Sciences, Chairman of the Erich Schmid Institute for Materials Science, Austria. Former Chairman of the International Institute for Applied Systems Analysis.
Prof Zihai Li	Centre for Immunotherapy of Cancer, University of Connecticut, USA.
Prof David Lloyd	Department of English, University of Southern California, USA.
Prof Hilbert Von Lohneysen	Physikalisches Institut, Universitat Karlsruhe, Germany.
Prof Chris Lowe	Director, Institute of Biotechnology, University of Cambridge, UK.
Prof Nona Lyons	Prof. of Education, Dartmouth College, New Hampshire, USA.
Prof Cora Marrett	Senior VP Academic Affairs, University of Wisconsin, USA.
Prof John F. Martin	Department of Medicine, University College London, UK.
Dr Polly Matzinger	Section Head, Laboratory of Cellular and Molecular Immunology, NIH, Bethesda, Maryland, USA.
Prof Robert M. Metzger	Laboratory for Molecular Electronics, University of Alabama, USA.
Prof Alan Michette	Department of Physics, King's College, London, UK.
Prof Michael Moran	Department of Government, University of Manchester, UK.
Prof Randall Mrsny	Professor of Drug Delivery, School of Pharmacy, Cardiff University, UK. Former Head of Drug Delivery, Genentech Inc. Founder and CSO of Trinity Biosystems Inc.
Prof Peter Nijkamp	Department of Regional Economics, The Free University, Amsterdam, The Netherlands.
Prof George O'Connor	Soil and Water Science Department, University of Florida, USA.
Prof Par Omling	Director General of the Swedish Research Council and Professor of Solid State Physics, Lund University, Sweden.
Dr Jonathan Pennock	Department of Natural Resources, University of New Hampshire, USA.
Prof Jennie Popay	Institute for Health Research, Lancaster University, UK.
Prof Eigil Praestgaard	Department of Life Sciences and Chemistry, Roskilde University, Denmark.
Prof Paul Rainey	School of Biological Sciences, University of Auckland, New Zealand.
Prof Katherine Richardson	Department of Marine Ecology, and currently Pro-Rector, University of Aarhus, Denmark.

Name	Affiliation
Prof Gordon C.K. Roberts	Director of the Biological NMR Centre and Head of Department of Biochemistry, University of Leicester, UK.
Prof Kevin J. Roberts	Department of Chemical Engineering, University of Leeds, UK.
Prof Stephen Robson	Department of Obstetrics & Gynaecology, Royal Victoria Infirmary, Newcastle upon Tyne, UK.
Prof Seppo Salminen	Professor of Food Development, University of Turku, Finland.
Prof Jim Smyth	Professor of History, University of Notre Dame, Indiana, USA.
Dr Hans Soderlund	Research Director, VTT Biotechnology, Finland
Rabbi Dr Sacha Stern	School for Oriental and African Studies, University of London, UK.
Mr Peter Stubley	Assistant Director, St. George's Library, University of Sheffield, UK.
Prof Georg Thallinger	Institute of Information Systems & Information Management, JOANNEUM RESEARCH Forschungsgesellschaft mbH, Austria.
Prof Christopher Vaughan	Director, MRC/UCT Medical Imaging Research Unit, Department of Human Biology, University of Cape Town, South Africa.
Dr Elisabeth Vestergaard	Senior Scientific Secretary for the Humanities, European Science Foundation and Research Director, The Danish Institute for Studies in Research and Research Policy, Aarhus, Denmark.
Prof Eric Vivier	Centre d'Immunologie de Marseille-Luminy et Département de Biologie, Faculté de Luminy, Université de la Méditerranée, Marseille, France.
Prof William Waites	Division of Food Science, University of Nottingham, UK.
Prof Bronwen Walter	Department of Applied Geography, Anglia Polytechnic University, UK.
Prof Joseph Wang	Regent Professor and Manasse Chair, Department of Chemistry and Biochemistry, New Mexico State University, USA.
Prof Horst Weller	Institut fuer Physikalische Chemie, Universitaet, Hamburg, Germany.
Mr David O. Williams	IT Division, CERN, Geneva, Switzerland.
Prof Martin Wills P	Department of Chemistry, University of Warwick, UK.
Prof Thomas M. Wilson	Department of Anthropology, Binghampton University, New York, USA.
Prof Eugene Wong	Emeritus Prof. Electrical and Computing Sciences, University College Berkeley, California, USA.

Name	Position
AIT	
Dr. Ciarán Ó Catháin	Director
Dr. Patrick Mulhern	Head of Development
Atlantic Philanthropies	
Mr. Colin McCrea	Senior Vice President
Biotrin Ireland	
Dr. Cormac Kilty	CEO/Chairman IBIA
CIT	
Mr Michael Delaney	Head of Development
DES	
Mr Paul Kelly	Assistant Secretary
Mr Kevin McCarthy	Principal Officer
Mr Ian McKenna	Assistant Principal
DETE	
Mr Ned Costello	Assistant Secretary
Mr Martin Shanagher	Principal Officer
Department of Finance	
Mr Jonathan Greer	NDP/CSF Evaluation Unit
Mr David Hegarty	NDP/CSF Evaluation Unit
Department of the Taoiseach	
Ms Mary Doyle	Assistant Secretary
DIAS	
Prof Luke Drury	Director Cosmogrid
DIT	
Prof Brian Norton	President
Ms Niomi Brant	UG
Dr Hugh Byrne	FOCAS Centre Director
Mr Allan Casey	UG
Dr Gordon Chambers	FOCAS/School of Physics
Dr Declan Glynn	Director External Affairs
Ms Katrina Haas	UG
Ms Louisa Hartnett	FOCAS administration
Dr Matt Hussey	Director Science Faculty
Dr Fiona Lyng	FOCAS PD
Dr Mary McNamara	FOCAS/School of Chemistry
Dr Alberto Morales	FOCAS PD
Dr Izabela Naydenova	FOCAS PD
Dr Noel Russell	FOCAS/Head of School of Chemistry
Dr Vincent Toal	FOCAS/Head of School of Physics
Dr Pat Walsh	FOCAS/School of Mathematical Science
DCU	
Prof Ferdinand von Prondzynski	President
Dr Danny O'Hare	Past President
Dr Prince Anandarajah	RINCE PD
Dr Liam Barry	RINCE/Department of Electronic Engineering
Mr Conor Bourke	PG
Dr Paul Clarke	NICB PD
Mr Martin Conry	Secretary
Ms Gene Dalton	UG
Ms Ada Diacones	PG
Prof Dermot Diamond	Vice President Research

Name	Position
Dr Jim Dowling	Head School of Engineering
Prof. Robert Forster	NCSR/Department of Chemical Sciences
Ms Kathleen Grennan	PG
Prof Eugene Kennedy	NCPST/Head of School of Physical Sciences
Mr Karol Kowalik	PG
Ms Sinead Loughran	PG
Ms Noleen Loughran	UG
Prof Brian MacCraith	Director, NCSR
Dr Tim McCormac	Department of Applied Science, IT Tallaght
Dr Aisling McEvoy	NCSR PD
Dr Gillian McMahon	Department of Analytical Chemistry
Prof Patrick McNally	Director RINCE
Dr Val Muresan	RINCE PD
Dr Noel Murphy	RINCE/School of Electronic Engineering
Dr Sean Murphy	RINCE PD
Dr Noel O'Connor	RINCE/School of Electronic Engineering
Prof Richard O'Kennedy	NICB/School of Biotechnology
Prof Albert Pratt	Deputy President DCU
Dr. Declan Raftery	Director, Office of the Vice President for Research
Dr Alec Reader	Research Officer, RINCE
Prof Malcolm Smyth	NCSR/School of Chemical Sciences
Mr Kieran Smyth	UG
Ms Caroline Toland	PG
Prof Miles Turner	Director NCPST
Dr Dermot Walls	NCSR/School of Biotechnology
Dr Paul Whelan	RINCE/School of Electronic Engineering
DMMC	
Dr. Pierre Meulien	Chief Executive, DMMC
Mr Arun Chandra	PG
Ms Ruth Foley	PG
Ms Áine Fox	PG
Prof Michael Gill	DMMC/Professor of Psychiartry, TCD
Prof Brian Harvey	DMMC/Professor of Molecular Medicine, RCSI
Prof Donal Hollywood	DMMC/Professor of Clinical Oncology, TCD
Dr Joe Keane	DMMC/Consultant Respiratory Physician
Prof Dermot Kelleher	DMMC/Professor of Clinical Medicine, TCD
Prof Mark Lawler	DMMC/Professor of Molecular Haematology, TCD
Dr Aideen Long	DMMC/Senior Lecturer, RCSI
Dr Christine Loscher	DMMC PD
Dr Patricia Maguire	DMMC PD
Dr Ross McManus	DMMC/Lecturer in Molecular Medicine, TCD
Dr Siobhan Mitchell	PD, DMMC

Note. Research collaborators are listed with the lead institution for a programme, and at the location at which they were met.

Name	Position
Ms Julie O'Brien	PG
Prof John Reynolds	DMMC/Department of Surgery, TCD
Dr Helen Roche	DMMC/Department of Clinical Medicine, TCD
Dr Yuri Vollov	DMMC/Department of Clinical Medicine, TCD

Dundalk IT

Name	Position
Mr Gerry Carroll	Head of Development

Enterprise Ireland

Name	Position
Mr Feargal Ó'Moráin	Director, Science and Innovation
Dr Martin Lyes	Manager, Science & Innovation
Dr Ena Prosser	Director Biotechnology Directorate
Dr John Smith	Research & Development, Innovation Management

Enterprise Strategy Group

Name	Position
Mr Eoin O Driscoll	Chairman Enterprise Strategy Group

EPA

Name	Position
Ms Lorraine Fegan	Programme Officer

FORFÁS

Name	Position
Mr. Martin Cronin	CEO
Mr. Michael Fitzgibbon	Manager, Indicators & Technical Evaluations Division
Mr. Declan Hughes	Manager, S&T Policy and Planning Division

GMIT

Name	Position
Dr. Marion Coy	Director
Mr. Andrew D'Arcy	Head of Development

HRB

Name	Position
Dr. Ruth Barrington	CEO
Ms Kay Duggan-Walls	Research Grants Officer

HEA

Name	Position
Dr. Don Thornhill	Chairman

IDA

Name	Position
Mr. Sean Dorgan	CEO
Mr. Peter Lillis	Manager, Education, Skills & Research Division
Mr. Eamonn Sheehy	Project Manager, Education, Skills & Research Division

ICSTI

Name	Position
Dr. Edward Walsh	Chairman ICSTI & Past President UL

IT Carlow

Name	Position
Ms Maebh Maher	Director
Mr. Brian Bennett	Registrar
Dr. Dina Brazil	Environmental Science/ Department of Applied Biology and Chemistry

Name	Position
Dr. David Dowling	Environmental Science/ Head of Department of Applied Biology and Chemistry
Dr. Linda Jennings	Environmental Science PD
Mr. Jim McEntee	External Services Manager
Dr. Patricia Mulcahy	Head of Development
Dr. Ger Murphy	Environmental Science/ Head of Department of Applied Biology and Chemistry
Mr. Cormac O'Toole	Secretary/Financial Controller
Dr. D. Ryan	Department of Applied Biology and Chemistry

Name	Position
Dr. Richard Thorn	Director
Mr Magus Amijirionwu	MSc
Dr. John Bartlett	Head of Research
Ms Mairese Feeney	UG
Mr. John Gault	Biosolids Research Programme/School of Science
Mr. Eamonn Grennan	Biosolids Research Programme/School of Science
Mr. Justin Lohan	UG
Mr. John McEvoy	UG
Mr. John McHugh	UG
Dr. Richard Moles	Department of Chemical & Environmental Sciences, UL
Ms Carmel Moran	MSc
Ms Ericka Murray	MSc
Prof. Tony Pembroke	UL
Mr. John O'Dea	Biosolids Research Programme/School of Science
Dr. Ted McGowan	Biosolids Research Programme/School of Science
Dr. Perry Share	Head of Department - Humanities
Dr. Pat Timpson	Head of School of Science

Name	Position
Dr. Henry Lyons	Head of Development

Name	Position
Mr. Jim O'Hara	General Manager

Name	Position
Dr. Chris Horn	Chairman & CEO

Name	Position
Mr. Brendan Butler	Director ICT Ireland

Name	Position
Mr. Matt Moran	Director

Name	Position
Prof Eda Sagarra	Chairman
Dr. Marc Caball	Director

Name	Position
IRCSET	
Prof. Tom Mitchell	Chairman
Mr. Martin Hynes	Director - The Embark Initiative
Irish Research Scientists Association	
Dr. Fiona Regan	Chair IRSA
MIC	
Ms Helen Gallagher	Research Office
NCAD	
Prof. Colm Ó Briáin	Director
Prof. Gary Granville	Head of Education
Mr. Ken Langan	Registrar
NUI Galway	
Prof. Iognáid Ó Muircheartaigh	President
Ms Orla Baxter	Development Officer
Dr. Colin Brown	ECI/Department Applied Geophysics
Dr. Miriam Byrne	ECI/Air Quality Technology Centre
Prof. Nicholas Canny	Director CSHSHC
Dr Helen Cantrell	PD ECI/Department of Political Science and Sociology
Dr William Carroll	NCBES/Department of Chemistry
Dr. Mary Cawley	ECI/Department of Geography
Prof. Emer Colleran	Director, ECI/Chair of Department of Microbiology
Ms. Karen Coughlan	UG
Mr. Gavin Collins	PG
Ms. Aoife Fenton	UG
Dr. William Golden	Department of Accountancy & Finance
Dr. Mike Gormally	ECI/Department of Microbiology
Prof. Michael Guirey	Director, MRI
Prof. Ger Hurley	Dean of Research
Prof. Gerard Jennings	ECI/ Department of Physics
Mr. Henry Kenny	UG
Dr. Su-Ming Khoo	ECI/Dept. Political Science & Sociology
Dr Christoph Kleefield	PD ECI/Department of Experimental and Applied Physics
Ms. Edel Larkin	UG
Ms. Emily McLucas	PG
Dr. Peter McHugh	NCBES/Department of Mechanical and Biomedical Engineering
Ms Elisabeth Matthews	UG
Dr. Karen Molloy	PD ECI/Department of Botany
Mr. James Moran	PG
Dr. Frederic Morand	PD ECI/Department of Economics
Dr. Patricia Morgan	Dean of Science
Dr. Bruce Murphy	PD NCBES/Department of Mechanical and Biomedical Engineering

Name	Position
Dr. Vincent O'Flaherty	ECI/Department Microbiology
Mr. Ronan O'Reilly	PG
Prof. Pádraig O'Donoghue	Dean of Engineering
Dr. Abhay Pandit	NCBES/Department of Mechanical and Biomedical Engineering
Dr. Martina Prendergast	Development Manager
Mr. Milosz Przyjalowski	PG
Dr. Lisa Pursell	PD ECI/Centre for Health Promotion Studies
Dr Iouri Rotchev	NCBES/Department of Mechanical and Biomedical Engineering
Dr. Alan Ryder,	NCBES/Department of Chemistry
Dr. Afshin Samali,	NCBES/Department Biochemistry
Dr. John Simmie	ECI/ Department of Chemistry
Prof. Terry Smith	Director NCBES
Dr. Catherine Stenson	PD NCBES/Department of Experimental Medicine and Pharmacology
Mr. Robert Wilkes	PG
NUI Maynooth	
Dr. William J. Smyth	President
Ms Linda Anderson	PD Institute of Immunology
Ms Claire Barry	UG
Ms Sarah Brennan	UG
Dr. David Casey	PD, Institute of Immunology
Dr. Derek Doherty	Institute of Immunology
Mr. Darren Ennis	PG
Ms Laura Estebas	PD, Institute of Immunology
Dr. Patricia Johnson	Institute of Immunology
Dr. Robert Kitchin	Director, NIRSA
Dr. Bernard Mahon	Director, Institute of Immunology
Prof. Frank Mulligan	Vice President of NUI Maynooth
Ms Cariosa Noone	PG
Dr. Tony O'Connor	PD Institute of Immunology
Dr. Shirley O'Dea	Institute of Immunology
Ms Mary O'Gorman	PG
Dr. Kay Ohlendieck	Head of Department of Biology
Mr. Raymond	Rowan UG
Dr. Jason Twamley	Dean of Research
Prof. James Walsh	Chairperson of Board of NIRSA, Head of Department of Geography
Ms Róisín McGowan	UG
RCSI	
Prof. Kevin O'Malley	Registrar/CEO
Ms Mary Alexander	Director of Finance
Dr. Gerard Cagney	Director of Proteomics
Prof. Dolores Cahill	IBS/Director, National Centre for Human Proteomics
Prof. Desmond Fitzgerald	Chairman of Clinical Pharmacology, Chair of the Health Research Board
Mr. Michael Horgan	Deputy Registrar/CEO

Name	Position
Prof. Dermot Kenny	IBS/Department of Clinical Pharmacology,
Dr. Terry McWade	Director, Office of Research & Technology Transfers
Dr. Niamh Moran	IBS/Department of Clinical Pharmacology
Dr. Phil O'Brien	Research Programmes Manager
Prof. Jochen Prehn	Head of Department of Physiology
Dr. Denis Shields	IBS/Institute of Bioinformatics
Dr. Achim Treumann	Director of Mass Spectrometry

St. Patricks College, Drumcondra

Name	Position
Dr. Pauric Travers	Director
Dr. Mary Shine-Thompson	College Research Co-ordinator

SFI

Name	Position
Dr. William C. Harris	Director General
Mr. Mattie McCabe	Director Corporate Affairs
Dr. Alastair Glass	Director ICT Division

Teagasc

Name	Position
Dr. Lance O'Brien	Head of Research Department

TCD

Name	Position
Prof. John Hegarty	Provost
Prof. Tom Mitchell	Past Provost
Mr. Robin Adams	Librarian Ussher Library
Ms Doris Alexander	Research Development Office
Prof. Werner Blau	Centre Director, IAMS
Prof. Vincent Cahill	IITAC/Department of Computer Science
Prof. Michael Coey	IAMS/ Department of Physics
Mr. Tim Cooper	Director of Buildings
Prof. John Corish	Director, IITAC/Department of Chemistry
Ms Catriona Creely	PG
Ms Audrey Crosbie	Business Development Manager, TCHPC
Prof. David Dickson	Director, Irish Scottish Studies/Department of Modern History
Dr. John Donegan	IAMS/Department of Physics
Ms Jane Finucane	PG
Ms Margaret Flood	Keeper, Ussher Library
Prof. Sean Freyne	Director, Mediterranean & Near Eastern Studies/School of Hebrew, Biblical & Theological Studies
Prof. Michael Gibney	Dean of Research
Prof. Sheila Greene	Senior Lecturer
Prof. Jane Grimson	Vice Provost
Dr. Yuri Gun'ko	IAMS/Department of Chemistry
Mr. Hugh Hayden	PG
Ms Arlene Healy	Sub-librarian, Ussher Library
Ms Karen Hosie	PG

Name	Position
Dr. Ben Jones	PD IAMS/Department of Physics
Prof. John Kelly	IAMS/Department of Chemistry
Ms Emer Kenny	UG
Dr. Philip Lane	Institute for International Integration Studies
Dr. Margaret Mahony	Transportation Research & Innovation for People
Ms Lidia Matasse	PG
Mr. Ian Mathews	Treasurers Office (Capital)
Prof. John McGilp	IAMS/Head of Department of Physics
Ms Louise McGuignan	UG
Ms Sharon McIntyre	Ussher Library
Dr. Alan Moore	Head of Micro-electronics
Dr. Carol O'Sullivan	IITAC/Department of Computer Science
Prof. John O'Hagan	Bursar
Dr. Shane O'Mara	Institute of Neuroscience
Dr. Eoin O'Neill	Director of Innovation Services
Mr. Trevor Peare	Keeper, Ussher Library
Dr. Suresh Pillai	PD IAMS
Prof. Patrick Prendergast	Centre for Bioengineering
Dr. Yury Rakovich	PD IAMS/Department of Physics
Ms Suzanne Richmond	PRTLI Administrator
Prof. John Saeed	Dean of Graduate Studies
Ms Deirdre Savage	Treasurers Office (Recurrent)
Prof. James Sexton	Director, IITAC/Department of Pure & Applied Mathematics
Ms Maria Treanor	Research Office
Ms Sonja Walker	UG
Dr. Graeme Watson	IITAC/Department of Chemistry
Dr. Margaret Woods	Technology Transfer Manager

UCC

Name	Position
Prof. Aidan Moran	Registrar
Prof. Kevin Collins	Vice President of UCC and Head of Department of Microbiology
Prof. Michael Mortell	Past President
Dr. Claire Adams	PD BSI/BIOMERIT
Dr. Joe Bogue	BSI/Department of Food Business and Development
Dr. Mark Carmody	PD BSI/Department of Biochemistry
Prof. Kevin Cashman	BSI/Department of Nutrition, Food and health
Prof. Tom Cotter	BSI/Department of Biochemistry
Prof. Gabriel Crean	Director, NMRC
Prof. Charles Daly	Biosciences Institute/ Faculty of Food Science and Technology
Dr. Conor Delahunty	Biosciences Institute/ Department of Food & Nutritional Sciences

Name	Position
Dr. Alan Dobson	Biosciences Institute/Department of Microbiology
Prof. Gerald Fitzgerald	Director, Research Programme in Food & Health
Mr. Rowan Flynn	PG
Prof. John Fraher	Director Bioscience Institute
Dr. James Greer	Director, Computational Modelling Group, NMRC
Dr. Paddy Harrison	Biosciences Institute/Department of Physiology
Dr. Colin Hill	Biosciences Institute/Department of Microbiology
Dr. Michael Keane	Biosciences Institute/Department of Food Business & Development
Ms Mary McCarthy	Biosciences Institute/Department of Food Business & Development
Dr. Kieran. McDermott	Biosciences Institute/Department of Anatomy
Dr. John Morgan	Biosciences Institute/Department of Microbiology
Ms Heidi Mulcahy	PG
Ms Deirdre Murphy	PG
Mr. Mike Nolan	PG
Dr. Nora O'Brien	Biosciences Institute/Department of Food & Nutritional Sciences
Dr. Rosemary O'Connor	Biosciences Institute/Department of Biochemistry
Ms Selena O'Keefe	PG
Dr. Alan O'Neill	NMRC
Mr. Brendan O'Neill	NMRC
Prof. Michael O'Sullivan	Vicepresident for Planning, Communications and Development
Dr. Aidan Quinn	NMRC
Dr. Gareth Redmond	Programme Director National Nanofabrication Facility
Prof. Yrjo Roos	Biosciences Institute/Head of Department of Food & Nutritional Sciences
Prof. Fergus Shanahan	Biosciences Institute/Professor and Chair of the Department of Medicine
Ms Michelle Sheehan	PG
Dr. Mark Tangney	Biosciences Institute/Cork Cancer Research Centre PD
Dr. Saskia van Ruth	Biosciences Institute/Department of Food Science and Technology
Dr. Douwe van Sinderen	Biosciences Institute/Department of Microbiology

UCD

Name	Position
Prof. Hugh Brady	President
Dr. Art Cosgrove	Past President
Dr. John Baugh	Conway Institute PD
Prof. Maurice Boland	Acting Vice President for Research
Ms Susan Butler	ISSC Manager
Dr. Arnaud Chevalier	ISSC/Department of Economics

Name	Position
Prof. John Coakley	ISSC/Department of Politics
Dr. Pádraig Conway	Vice President for Communications Development
Ms Niamh Cosgrave	PG
Dr. Mary Daly	Director HII
Dr. Paul Daly	Conway Institute PD
Mr. Charlie Delap	PG
Dr. Kevin Denny	ISSC/Department of Economics
Dr. Seamus Donnelly	Deputy Director IMM
Ms Claire Finn	PG
Dr. Joanne Gallagher	Conway Institute PD
Ms Gladys Ganiel	PG
Prof. Catherine Godson	Vice President for Innovation & Corporate Partnerships
Dr. Pat Guiry	Conway Institute/Department of Chemistry
Dr. Niamh Hardiman	ISSC/Department of Politics
Dr. Colm Harmon	Director, ISSC
Prof. Des Higgins	Professor of Bioinformatics, Conway Institute
Ms Carol Laffan	PG
Prof. Finian Martin	Conway Institute/Associate Professor of Pharmacology
Prof. Paul McLoughlin	Conway Institute/Associate Professor of Physiology
Prof. Peter Neary	ISSC/Professor of Political Economy
Dr. Philip Nolan	Acting Director of the Conway Institute
Ms Niamh O'Sullivan	PG
Prof. Stephen Pennington	Conway Institute/Professor of Proteomics
Prof. Michael Ryan	Conway Institute/Department of Pharmacology
Prof. Richard Sinnott	ISSC/Associate Professor of Politics
Ms Laura Thornton	PG
Dr. R. William Watson	Conway Institute/Department of Surgery
Dr. John Yarwood	Director, Urban Institute

UL

Name	Position
Dr. Roger Downer	President
Prof. Noel Buckley	MSSI/Department of Physics
Mr. Jason Clohessy	PG
Prof. Vincent Cunnane	Vice President Research
Dr. Teresa Curtin	MSSI/Department of Chemical and Environmental Sciences
Prof. Stuart Hampshire	MSSI/Department of Materials Science and Technology
Prof. Kieran Hodnett	MSSI/Department of Chemical and Environmental Sciences
Dr. Mitch Loan	MSSI PD
Dr. Edmond Magner	Director, MSSI
Dr. Tim McGloughlin	MSSI/Department of Mechanical and Aeronautical Engineering
Dr. Miroslav Mihov	MSSI PD
Ms Siobhán O'Callaghan	PG

Name	Position
Mr. Leonard O'Mahony	PG
Prof. Tony Pembroke	Head, Department of Chemical & Environmental Sciences
Prof. Michael Pomeroy	MSSI/Department of Materials Science and Technology
Dr. Marina Serantoni	MSSI PD
Dr. Ken Stanton	MSSI/Department of Materials Science and Technology
WIT	
Prof. Kieran Byrne	Director
Dr. Willie Donnelly	Head of Research
Dr. Eric Martin	Head of School of Science
Dr. Venie Martin	Head of Development and Postgraduate Studies
Mr. John McConnell	Vice Director
Wyeth Medica	
Dr. Reg Shaw	Managing Director
Dr. Brendan Hughes	Director of Development

HEA MEMBERS

Chairman:

Dr. Don Thornhill,
Higher Education Authority.

Professor Tom Boylan
Department of Economics,
National University of Ireland, Galway

Dr. Maurice Bric,
Department of Modern History,
University College Dublin.

Mr. William James Caves,
Former Chief Executive, Northern Ireland Schools
Examinations and Assessment Council (CCEA)

Cllr. Maria Corrigan,
Member, Dún Laoghaire Rathdown County Council

Mr. Martin Cronin,
Chief Executive, Forfás

Dr. Honor Fagan,
Department of Sociology, NUI Maynooth

Ms Maura Grant
Director of Programmes relating to Educational
Disadvantage, Department of Education and Science

Professor Gary Granville
Faculty of Education,
National College and Art and Design

Ms Carol Marie Herron,
Education Co-ordinator,
Co. Cavan VEC and Cavan Partnership

Mr. Paul Hannigan
Director, Letterkenny Institute of Technology

Mr. Patrick J. Kirby
Group Commercial Director, Alphyra

Ms Monica Leech
Communications Consultant

Professor Tom McCarthy
Professor of Economics and Dean of Business School,
Dublin City University

Ms Antoinette Nic Gearailt
Principal, The Donahies Community School, Dublin

Mr. Barry O'Brien,
Director (Estate and Support Services),
Royal College of Surgeons in Ireland

Professor Sarah Moore,
Dean of Teaching and Learning, University of Limerick

Professor Ciaran Murphy,
Department of Accounting , Finance & Information Systems,
University College Cork

Mr. Will Priestley,
President, Union of Students in Ireland

HEA EXECUTIVE

SECRETARY/CHIEF EXECUTIVE	Tom Boland
DEPUTY CHIEF EXECUTIVE	Mary Kerr
HEAD OF POLICY AND PLANNING	Fergal Costello
HEAD OF RESEARCH PROGRAMMES	Dr. Eucharia Meehan
HEAD OF ADMINISTRATION	Padraic Mellett
HEAD OF INFORMATION AND PUBLIC AFFAIRS	Gerry O'Sullivan
HEAD OF NATIONAL OFFICE FOR EQUITY OF ACCESS TO HIGHER EDUCATION	Dr Mary-Liz Trant
MANAGEMENT ACCOUNTANT	Stewart Roche
ASSISTANT SECRETARY	Mary Armstrong - *Recurrent Grants*
ASSISTANT SECRETARY	Sheena Duffy - *Research,Socrates /Erasmus*
ASSISTANT SECRETARY	Jennifer Gygax - *Recurrent Grants*
ASSISTANT SECRETARY	George Ryan- *Physical Development*
ASSISTANT SECRETARY	Orla Christle- *National Office*
ASSISTANT SECRETARY	Peter Brown- *National Office*
HEAD OF ICT SKILLS PROJECT TEAM	Pat O'Connor

SENIOR POLICY ANALYST POLICY AND PLANNING   Caitriona Ryan

STATISTICS SECTION
Barbara Carr
Oliver Mooney
Frank Condon

INFORMATION AND PUBLIC AFFAIRS
Cliona Buckley

POLICY AND PLANNING
Leonora Harty
Rowena Dwyer

RECURRENT GRANTS
Jane Sweetman
Mary May
Valerie Harvey

INDUSTRIAL RELATIONS UNIT
Maura O'Shea
Justin Sinnott

EUROPEAN PROGRAMMES
Louise Sherry
Adrian O'Donoghue

RESEARCH PROGRAMMES
Dr. Lisa Higgins
Dr. Emer Cunningham
Eileen O'Connell
Fiona Davis
Adrian O'Donoghue

PHYSICAL DEVELOPMENT
Ciaran Dolan
Patricia Carroll
Brendan Ferron

HEA EXECUTIVE

PERSONNEL AND ACCOUNTS

Niall O'Connell

Emer McMullin

Sharon O'Rourke

SECRETARIAL SERVICES

Jacintha Healy *(Secretary to Chairman)*

Mary Dunne *(Secretary to Secretary/Chief Executive)*

Mary Meade

Kate Philbin-Dargan

INFORMATION TECHNOLOGY

John Muldoon, IT Manager

Marie O'Sullivan, LAN Administrator

NATIONAL OFFICE FOR EQUITY OF ACCESS TO HIGHER EDUCATION

Olive Walsh

Alan McGrath

Brian Johnston

Justin Synnott

Modesta Mawarire

RECEPTION

Shauna Brennan *(Marine House)*

Graham Barry *(Brooklawn House)*

SERVICES

Bridget Kelly

Caroline Curtis